Hg2 Lisbon

A Hedonist's guide to
Lisbon

BY Sarah Marshall
PHOTOGRAPHY Sarah Marshall

A Hedonist's guide to Lisbon

Managing director – Tremayne Carew Pole
Series editor – Catherine Blake
Production – Navigator Guides
Design – P&M Design
Typesetting – Dorchester Typesetting
Repro – PDQ Digital Media Solutions Ltd
Printers – Printed in Italy by Printer Trento srl
PR – Ann Scott
Publisher – Filmer Ltd

Email – info@ahedonistsguideto.com
Website – www.ahedonistsguideto.com

First published in the United Kingdom in 2004 by
Filmer Ltd
47 Filmer Road,
London SW6 7JJ

ISBN – 0-9547878-5-4

Hg2 Lisbon

CONTENTS

How to...	6
Updates	6
The concept	7
Lisbon	8
LISBON MAP	10
LISBON BY AREA	
BAIXA/BAIRRO ALTO	12
AVENIDA/RATO/ESTRÊLA	16
GRAÇA/SÉ/ALFAMA	20
LAPA/ALCÂNTARA/BELÉM	24
SLEEP	28
EAT	58
DRINK	98
SNACK	124
PARTY	148
CULTURE	168
SHOP	182
PLAY	194
INFO	204

How to…

A Hedonist's guide to… is broken down into easy to use sections: Sleep, Eat, Drink, Snack, Party, Culture, Shop, Play and Info. In each of these sections you will find detailed reviews and photographs.

At the front of the book you will find an introduction to the city and an overview map, followed by introductions to the four main areas and more detailed maps. On each of these maps you will see the places that we have reviewed, laid out by section, highlighted on the map with a symbol and a number. To find out about a particular place, simply turn to the relevant section where all entries are listed alphabetically.

Alternatively, browse through a specific section (i.e. Eat) until you find a restaurant that you like the look of. Next to your choice will be a small coloured dot – each colour refers to a particular area of the city – then simply turn to the relevant map to discover the location.

Updates

Due to the lengthy publishing process and shelf lives of books it is very difficult to keep travel guides up to date – new restaurants, bars and hotels open up all the time, while others simply fade away or just go out of style. What we can offer you are free updates– simply log onto our website www.ahedonistsguideto.com or www.hg2.net and enter your details, answer a question to provide proof of purchase and you will be entitled to free updates for a year from the date that you sign up. This will enable you to have all the relevant information at your finger tips whenever you go away.

In order to help us with this any comments that you might have, or recommendations that you would like to see in the guide in future please feel free to email us at info@ahedonistsguideto.com.

The concept

A Hedonist's guide to... is designed to appeal to a more urbane and stylish traveller. The kind of traveller who is interested in gourmet food, elegant hotels and seriously chic bars – the traveller who feels the need to explore, shop and pamper themselves away from the madding crowd.

Our aim is to give you the inside knowledge of the city, to make you feel like a well-heeled, sophisticated local and to take you to the most fashionable places in town to rub shoulders with the local glitterati.

In today's world work rules our life, weekends away are few and far between, and when we do go away we want to have the most fun and relaxation possible with the minimum of stress. This guide is all about maximizing time. Everywhere is photographed, so before you go you know exactly what you are getting into; choose a restaurant or bar that suits you and your demands.

We pride ourselves on our independence and our integrity. We eat in all the restaurants, drink in all the bars and go wild in the nightclubs – all totally incognito. We charge no one for the privilege for appearing in the guide, every place is reviewed and included at our discretion.

We feel cities are best enjoyed by soaking up the atmosphere and the vibrancy; wander the streets, indulge in some retail relaxation therapy, re-energize yourself with a massage and then get ready to eat like a king and party hard in the stylish local scene.

We feel that it is important for you to explore a city on your own terms, while the places reviewed provide definitive coverage in our eyes; one's individuality can never be wholly accounted for. Whatever you do we can assure you that you will have an unforgettable weekend.

Lisbon

Out on a limb both geographically and financially (and politically, up until 30 years ago), Portugal has always been considered the European outsider. But that image is now changing. Both Expo '98 and the Euro 2004 football championships have helped boost the country's international profile beyond that of a last-minute bucket holiday destination. The epicentre of this cultural transformation is Lisbon. At one time unjustly overlooked, this small but fiercely dynamic city has rightfully earned a place in the European capital super-league. Attracted by the prospect of relatively uncharted territory, city break travellers are now flocking for a taste of Rio in the Med.

It's hard to believe that up until 1974 Portugal was governed by a quasi-fascist dictatorship (Europe's last, in fact). But in the past 30 years a rapidly growing liberal and consumer society has evolved, and Lisbon has not looked back. This change is most evident on the cobbled streets of Bairro Alto, where a plethora of historically illegal drinking dens now forms the nucleus for much of the city's vibrant nightlife. Locals and tourists of all shapes, sizes and walks of life gather every Friday and Saturday night for what could quite conceivably be Europe's biggest bar crawl. With a reputation to rival that of São Paulo, Lisboetas love to party.

The Portuguese are famed for their love of eating and no self-respecting Lisboeta would even consider hitting the town without first sitting down to dinner. Eating forms a pivotal part of the social scene and you'll find more restaurants per square mile than street lamps. Consequently the demand for quality (and quantity) is high. Be warned: it won't be just your suitcases that get tagged for excess baggage.

The city itself is small enough to explore in a weekend, although it's easy to get lost in the narrow, cobbled backstreets. Perhaps the best way to find your bearings is to climb one of the city's seven hills and take in the breathtaking views. Areas are concentrated and boast their own defined character; discover the charm of Lisbon's oldest *bairro*, the Alfama, where old women nonchalantly watch the world pass by from their window boxes; or the cultural district of Belém, where many of the city's museums and historic buildings are located. The Castelo de São Jorge serves as a good vantage-point for some of the most beautiful sunsets in Europe, with a mystical light to rival that of Venice.

Lisbon is a city of contradictions, where wealth and poverty live as comfortable neighbours, and modernity meets with unwavering tradition – making it both a charming and intriguing place to explore. Behind the crumbling stonework, a new spirit is evolving. Once a leading world power, Lisbon now looks likely to resume some of its former glory. As the locals would put it – this city will touch you.

☕ SNACK

1. Antiga Confeitaria
   de Belém
23. Pasteis de Cerveja
24. Pastelaria Versailles

⬤ PARTY

22. Showgirls

AVENIDA

CAMPOLIDE

CAMPO DE
OURIQUE

RATO

BAIRRO DO
ALVITO

ALCÂNTARA / LAPA

LAPA

ALCÂNTARA

RIO TEJO

0   0.5   1 km

Lisbon city map

SLEEP

4. Carlton Pestana Palace
12. Hotel Real Palácio
21. Quinta Nova da Conceição
22. Sheraton Lisboa

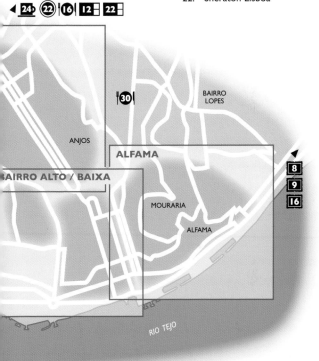

CULTURE

2. Centro de Arte Moderna
6. Mosteiro dos Jerónimos
7. Museu do Design
8. Museu Nacional do Azulejo
9. Ocenarium
10. Torre de Belém
11. Centro Cultural de Belém
14. Fundação Calouste Gulbenkian
16. Teatro Luís de Camões

 EAT

5. Aya
14. Estufa Real
16. Galeto
30. Ramiro

Baixa/Bairro Alto

The Baixa area of downtown Lisbon is characterized by a rigorous grid system. Following a devastating earthquake in 1755, much of the original medieval city was destroyed. The King's minister Marquês de Pombal, now a national hero, rebuilt the area using a neo-classical system of urban planning. Each road was assigned a different trade or craft, to which current street names still bear testimony: Rua Aurea ('gold road') is still the place to find jewellers, while Rua dos Sapateiros is a 'street of shoe-makers'.

For many visitors, the Baixa is their first encounter with Lisbon. Tourist restaurants cluster along the side streets and many traditional shops are still open for trade. Praca Dom Pedro IV, or Rossio, as it is better known, forms a focal point in the city both geographically and socially; its baroque fountains and mosaic paving (still restored by hand) are a useful landmark from any of the city's *miradouros* (look-out points). A constant stream of taxis passes through the square, and it's a popular spot for shoe-cleaners, chestnut sellers and street performers.

People seem to hang around street corners from dawn until dusk doing nothing in particular. Many are immigrants and unemployed – victims of Portugal's ongoing economic crisis. They are largely harmless, but don't be surprised if a crafty salesman offers you a pair of stolen sunglasses or a block of hashish.

Neighbouring Chiado is a district of theatres, cafés and fashion boutiques. It was once the centre of Lisbon's intellectual life; the city's oldest bookshop, Livraria Bertrand, can be found on the Largo do Chiado along with Café a Brasílieira, once a haunt of writer Fernando Pessoa.

According to legend, the area is named after 16th-century poet Antonio Ribeiro, nicknamed 'O Chiado' (meaning 'squeaking' or 'hissing'). Rua Garrett forms the main drag of shops, although boutiques are dotted around the side streets. The area was engulfed by a fire in 1988; the reconstruction, overseen by Oporto architect Alvaro Siza Vieira, is in keeping with Chiado's tradition of grand marble façades.

The Bairro Alto (upper town) lies to the west of the city centre. It was the first district in Lisbon to have straight and regular streets, but they are nothing like as regimented as Baixa's. Narrow cobbled roads and dead ends make it a confusing place to uncover. A crowd of young bohemians moved into the undamaged *bairro* following the 1755 earthquake and their legacy remains to this day. Rua do Século and Rua do Diário de Notícias are named after the daily papers that once had their offices on these streets.

Since the 1980s the crumbling back alleys have taken on a Jekyll and Hyde personality. By day greengrocers quietly go about their business, while old women share conversations across heavily laundry-laden balconies. The quiet streets are largely residential, although the city's young design elite have moved in and opened several boutiques, housing alternative fashion. Trendy tattoo parlours, art shops and bakeries are also open for business. The only bar open before dark is Side.

As night falls, a complete transformation takes place. Shop shutters close, bar doorways open and the sound of pints being pulled replaces the clunking of old-fashioned cash registers. Dormant by day, a plethora of backstreet bars breathe life into the sleepy *bairro*. Revellers arrive in their droves and hop from venue to venue. Most gather in the streets outside, creating a scene resembling a summer festival. The city's greatest concentration of restaurants can also be found here – ranging from the traditional to cosmopolitan, and expensive to budget. There are plenty of *fado* houses all vying for attention and owners have no qualms about accosting tourists. For the most part, however, they are tacky amusement arcades.

EAT

I.	I de Maio	24.	Olivers
8.	Casa Nostra	26.	Pap' Açorda
II.	Charcuteria	29.	Primavera
12.	El Gordo	32.	Sinal Vermelho
19.	Lisboa Noite	37.	Tavares Rico

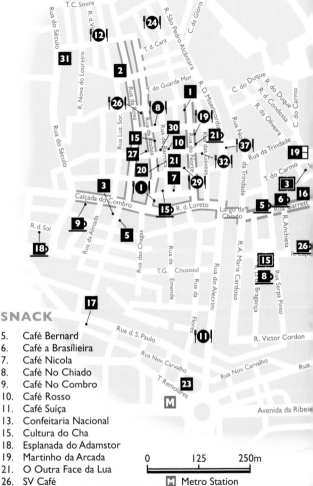

SNACK

5.	Café Bernard
6.	Café a Brasílieira
7.	Café Nicola
8.	Café No Chiado
9.	Café No Combro
10.	Café Rosso
11.	Café Suíça
13.	Confeitaria Nacional
15.	Cultura do Cha
18.	Esplanada do Adamstor
19.	Martinho da Arcada
21.	O Outra Face da Lua
26.	SV Café

0   125   250m

M Metro Station

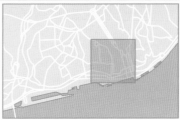

SLEEP

11.   Hotel Metropole
15.   Lisboa Regency Chiado
16.   Lisboa Tejo Hotel
19.   Olissipo

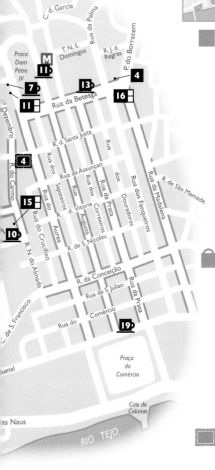

DRINK

1.   121
2.   Agito
3.   Baliza
4.   Berim Bar
5.   Bicaense
7.   Cafédiário
10.   Clube da Esquina
15.   Fragil
16.   Herois
17.   Lounge Café
20.   Majong
21.   Mexe
23.   O' Gilins
27.   Portas Largas
30.   Side
31.   Snob

SHOP

Rua do Carmo
Largo do Chiado
Rua Augusto
Rua da Atalaia
Rua da Aurea
Rua da Betesga
Rua da Conceicao
Rua da Madalena
Rua da Prata
Rua da Rosa
Rua do Loreto
Rua do Norte

CULTURE

3.   Convento do Carmo
4.   Elevador da Santa Justa
15.   Teatro Nacional de Sao Carlos

Avenida/Rato/Estrêla

Described by Fernando Pessoa as 'the finest artery in Lisbon', the 90-metre-wide Avenida da Liberdade connects the 18th-century downtown with 19th-century areas. Based on the Champs-Elysees, it was completed in 1886. The leafy boulevard is a busy thoroughfare for traffic, lined with towering office blocks and designer fashion stores. Lisbon's hotel district sprawls along this stretch, with a mixture of high-rise chains and more historic premises.

At the bottom of the Avenida lies the neo-Manueline Rossio station, with its tremendous horse-shoe archways. At the top, the busy Marquês de Pombal roundabout opens to the north of the city and Lisbon's business district. The 19th-century Parque Eduardo VII is an austerely landscaped open space, lacking any distinctive charm. The city bullring (currently undergoing renovation) and Benfica stadium can be found in the sprawling suburbs to the north of the city.

Located roughly halfway along the Avenida is Praça da Alegria, once a notorious red-light district. Today, only a few down-market strip-joints remain, although many of the decaying façades are still intact. Buried amid these is the city's oldest jazz bar, Hot Clube. A tortuously steep stairwell leads from a former aqueduct (now trendy restaurant/wine bar Enoteca) to the leafy parkland of Principe Real. This peaceful and

leafy romantic setting is also a popular gay and lesbian hang-out.

Make your way down to Pão de Canela in nearby Praça das Flores for a little rest and contemplation over a cup of coffee. A design community has grown up around this spot and houses some of the city's most innovative homeware and furniture shops. The Rua de O Século runs south into Bairro Alto and is home to a number of art galleries and creative spaces.

The Portuguese parliament building, a former Benedictine monastery, dominates the neighbourhood of São Bento. Aside from a few up-market restaurants and bars (Galeria, Café de São Bento) it's a quiet area at night. The Rua de São Bento boasts Portugal's highest concentration of antique shops – from classic furnishings to knick-knacks and curios. The area around Rua do Poço dos Negros ('well of the negroes') is rather less salubrious, but home to a lively African community.

To the north-west of the city lie Estrêla and Campo de Ourique, middle-class districts. The Jardim da Estrêla, with swan pond and playground, is a pleasant park space. The areas are largely residential, the most famous former inhabitant being poet Fernando Pessoa. Restaurants worth a visit are XL and Tasquina de Adelaide. Two smoky black-glass towers pinpoint the Amoreiras business district beyond. Far more pleasant surroundings can be found in the shady Jardim das Amoreiras, beneath the arches of the Aquaducto das Águas Livres.

17 **38**

Parque Eduardo VII

7

Rua Castilho

5

Rua Joaquim A. d. Aguiar

14

Ⓜ

6

21

Rua Castilho

Rua Braancamp

Avenida da Liberdade

9

Rua Alexandre Herculano

5 **28**

8

26

25

Ⓜ

13

Rua de São Bento

3

Rua da Escola Politécnica

17

13

16

Rua

25

22

25 **25**

Rua do Século

🛍 **SHOP**

- ■ Avenida da Liberdade
- ■ Rua Dom Pedro V
- ■ Rua da Escola Politécnica
- ■ Rua do São Bento
- ■ Rua do Século

0   250   500m

Ⓜ Metro Station

SNACK

3. AS Vicentinhas
4. Buenas Aires
14. Crazy Nuts
16. Esplanada
22. Pão de Canela
25. Pastelaria Padaria
    São Roque

PARTY

17. Hot Clube

SLEEP

3. Avenida Palace
5. Dom Pedro Hotel Lisboa
6. Fenix Lisboa
7. Four Seasons Hotel Ritz
8. Hotel Altis
9. Hotel Britania
10. Hotel Lisboa Plaza
13. Hotel Venezia
17. Le Meridien Park Atlantic
18. NH Liberdade
25. Tivoli Jardim
26. Tivoli Lisboa
28. VIP Eden

DRINK

25. Pavilhão Chinês
28. Procópio

CULTURE

5. Mãe de Água
13. Coliseu dos Recreios
16. Teatro Nacional
    Dona Maria II

EAT

13. Enoteca
17. Gambrinus
21. Mezza Luna
27. Pinoquio
38. Varanda Restaurant

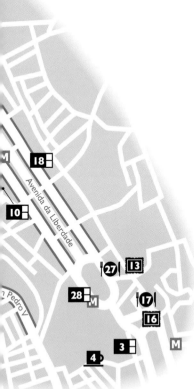

Graça/Sé/Alfama

Some of Lisbon's most beautiful historic monuments can be found east of Baixa in the sleepy Sé and Castelo districts. An air of peace and tranquillity prevails in this traditional city quarter. Take the winding 28 tram to gain a real sense of the space.

The 12th-century Sé cathedral, founded on the site of the city's main mosque, was built to commemorate Lisbon's liberation from the Moors and is a key landmark. Several bars and restaurants (Viagem des Sabores, Divína Comédia) nestle beneath the Romanesque structure.

A further hike leads to the Castelo de São Jorge, a hilltop fortification predating the Romans. This was the site of Lisbon's first Iron Age settlement, which was subsequently also bequeathed a degree of cultural heritage by the Visigoths and Moors. The castle walls are popular with lovers taking an evening stroll, and are a great place to watch the sun set.

Some of the city's most atmospheric and unique hotels can be found in this part of town: Solar do Castelo lies within the city walls, while

Palácio Belmonte is an ambitious palace conversion. Although not known for its social life, the area has a number of pleasant bars and cafés that have opened on the Costa do Castelo road circumnavigating São Jorge; the Chapitô circus school and social collective exemplify the bohemian and artistic character of the neighbourhood.

Residential life resumes in the gentle but bustling Graça neighbourhood. Panoramic views from the Largo da Graça are some of the best Lisbon has to offer and attract a meandering Sunday afternoon crowd. The Feira da Ladra flea market takes place on Tuesdays and Saturdays in the Campo de Santa Clara, which also houses a well-respected loft-space restaurant.

The oldest and most densely populated of Lisbon's *bairros* is the Alfama. The name 'Al-hama' is Arabic for 'fountain', and the pattern of blind alleys, winding stairways and twisting paths is Moorish. It's a veritable rabbit warren, and many streets barely register on the map. A local community continues to live in rent-controlled but dilapidated buildings. After dark the melancholic sound of *fado* spills from authentic *tascas* – an appropriate soundtrack for desperate tourists lost in the maze of backstreets. Cars have restricted access, so exploration by foot is essential. Look out for mischievous children who like to roam the streets at night in search of trouble.

Directly on the waterfront lies the trendy Santa Apolónia development, where selective design shops and restaurants bask in peaceful surroundings. Owned by style guru Manuel Reis and John Malkovich, both club Lux and restaurant Bica do Sapato come highly recommended.

SHOP

🔳 Santa Apolonia

SLEEP

1. Albergaria Senhora do Monte
20. Palácio Belmonte
23. Solar do Castelo
24. Solar dos Mouros

Graça/Sé/Alfama   local map

PARTY

9. Lux
16. Clube de Fado

0   125   250m

M Metro Station

CULTURE

1. Castelo de São Jorge
12. Chapitô

EAT

6. Bica do Sapato
9. Casanova
10. Chapitô
20. Mercado de Santa Clara
25. Os Corvos
31. Santo Antonio
35. Sushi Bar
39. Viagem de Sabores

DRINK

8. Caxim
9. Costa do Castelo Bar des Imagens
11. Divina Comédia
22. Net Jazz Café
29. Santiago Alquimista

SNACK

2. Arte Café
12. Cerca Moura
17. Esplanada da Graça
27. Teatro Taborda
28. Verde Perto

Lapa/Alcântara/Belém

Much of Lisbon's wealth is concentrated in Lapa, to the west of São Bento. A moneyed set live alongside the diplomatic community in palaces that betray Lisbon's aristocratic past. Unfortunately, laws governing rent control mean that landlords are reluctant to invest in much-needed improvements, and once-glorious buildings now crumble in neglect. Apart from a few cafés, this is a largely residential area. Several up-market hotels can be found along Rua das Janelas Verdes (York House and As Janelas Verdes), while the Lapa Palace enjoys some of the most luxurious facilities in town.

The warehouse superclubs and raucous bars of the infamous *docas* developments are just a stone's throw away from Lapa. A string of nightclubs along Santos and the Avenida 24 de Julho range from the 'tolerable' to 'best avoided'. Kapital serves a wealthy crowd, while Kremlin attracts an interesting psycho-geographical mix, all steeped in a life of grime. Cross the busy dual carriageway to reach Rocha Conde d'Óbidos. Bathed in neon, these cut-price commercial clubs are the first port of call for out-of-towners. Slightly more up-market restaurants and clubs can be found west of the flyover underneath the Ponte 25 de Abril suspension bridge. Running parallel to the train tracks and a dual carriageway, the stretch from Cais do Sodré to Alcântara can feel empty and soulless. It's a stark contrast to the intimacy of Bairro Alto.

A visit to Belém will give tourists a whistle-stop introduction to Lisbon's historic past and contemporary culture. It's just a 10-minute tram ride from Praça do Comercio, so it's hard to believe the district was once considered a separate entity ('Restelo'). Sights worth seeing include the Manueline Torre de Belém (one of Lisbon's most recognizable symbols) and the CCB – a modern performance space with adjoining design museum. Now a successful marina, the port played a valuable role in Portuguese maritime achievements: Christopher Columbus stopped here in 1493 on his way back to Spain after his discovery of the Americas, and in 1497 Vasco da Gama set off to discover a maritime route to India. The Padrão dos Descobrimentos ('Monument to the Discoveries') recalls their achievements.

On Sundays the open lawns and esplanades are seething with visitors. Head to the tropical gardens of Jardim do Ultramarino to escape the madding crowds. A visit to the Antiga Casa de Pasteis de Belém is also compulsory; Lisboetas regularly make a pilgrimage here to buy the speciality *pasteis de Belém* (custard tarts). The Pasteis de Cerveja, serving beer cakes, is another popular choice but the cakes themselves are not quite so tasty. Above Belém lies the Palacio da Ajuda, now home to the Culture Ministry, and beyond that the vast pine forest of Monsanto. Millions of trees were planted on the hillsides in the 1930s and the area is now referred to as the 'lung' of Lisbon. Although the area accounts for an eighth of the city, it offers very few attractions for the visitor.

PARTY

1. B. Leza
2. BBC
3. Convento
4. Docks Club
5. Incognito
6. Kapital
7. Kremlin
8. Lontra
10. O2Lx
11. Op Art
12. Paradise Garage
13. People
14. Queens
15. W
18. Senhor Vinho
19. Speakeasy
20. Champagne Club
21. Savana

SLEEP

2. AS Janelas Verdes
14. Lapa Palace
27. Vila Galé Opera
29. York House

SHOP

Rua de São Bento

0   250   500m

M Metro Station

SNACK

20. O Cha da Lapa

DRINK

6. Café de São Bento
12. Esplanada do Rio
13. Estado Liquido
14. Fluid
18. Lua
19. Madres de Goa
24. Paródia
26. Perudiguous do Rio

EAT

2. Alcântra Café
3. A Picanha
4. A Travessa
7. Bolshoi
15. Galeria
18. Kais
22. Nariz Apurado
23. Nariz do Vinho Tinto
28. Porco Pretto
33. Solar dos Nunes
34. Sua Excelencia
36. Tasquina da Adelaide
40. XL

sleep...

Although there are plenty of hotels in Lisbon, only a handful are of a really discernable quality. However, in the past two years many of the big chain hotels have invested in large-scale improvements, elevating their status beyond the city standard. Two prime examples are the Fenix and Meridian, whose style-friendly face-lifts have merited their inclusion in this book.

Most multi-storey hotels can be found around the Avenida da Liberdade, a short stroll from Lisbon's designer boutiques. Many can be impersonal, but guarantee a reliable range of facilities. The Four Seasons Ritz and NH Liberdade are the best hotels along this stretch.

More characteristic hotels can be found further afield in wealthy Lapa or contemplative Castelo. Those in search of regal surroundings can choose from several hotels housed within former palace walls (Lapa Palace, Carlton Pestana Palace, Hotel Real Palácio, Belmonte and Avenida Palace). Currently regarded as the city's top hotel, the Carlton Pestana Palace is easily the most impressive. The wonderfully landscaped Lapa Palace comes a close second. If you've got money to burn and an appetite for the obscure, the Belmonte comes highly recommended. A cheaper but equally unique alternative just down the road is

Solar dos Mouros. An entirely different experience can be had at the Quinta Nova da Conceição, an 18th-century country guesthouse north of the city in Benfica.

One chain to look out for is the family-run Hoteis Heritage, which looks after As Janelas Verdes, Hotel Britania, Hotel Lisboa Plaza and Solar do Castelo. These hotels each possess their own welcoming charm and are of a consistently high quality. Guests are encouraged to use a self-service bar, which is a trusting (but dangerous) touch. The Lisboa Regency Chiado and Lisboa Tejo represent a new wave of design hotels and combine a convenient location with good taste.

All hotels included in this section have their own bathrooms, and prices quoted range from a single in low season to a suite in high season. Many chains often have seasonal deals, so it's worth checking ahead. A good proportion of hotels also provide twin beds in place of doubles – apparently in response to a demand from the northern European market.

Our top ten hotels in Lisbon are:
1. Palácio Belmonte
2. Solar do Castelo
3. Lapa Palace
4. Carlton Pestana Palace
5. Lisboa Regency Chiado
6. Solar dos Mouros
7. York House
8. Lisboa Tejo Hotel
9. Four Seasons Hotel Ritz
10. NH Liberdade

Our top five hotels for style are:
1. Palácio Belmonte
2. Carlton Pestana Palace
3. Solar do Castelo
4. Lapa Palace
5. Lisboa Regency Chiado

Our top five hotels for atmosphere are:
1. Palácio Belmonte
2. Carlton Pestana Palace
3. York House
4. Solar do Castelo
5. Quinta Nova da Conceição

Our top five hotels for location:
1. Lisboa Regency Hotel
2. Lisboa Tejo Hotel
3. VIP Eden
4. Avenida Palace
5. Hotel Metrópole

Albergaria Senhora Do Monte, Calçada do Monte 39 (Miradouro da Senhora do Monte), Graça.
Tel: 21 886 6002 www.maisturismo.pt
Rates: €85–175

This hilltop pensão opened in 1969 and little has changed since. The formica floors and pine veneer panels of the lobby are deliciously tacky. It's a look retro obsessives would pay thousands to re-create. Rooms are simple, but clean and bright. Several have private balconies with fantastic views of the city and the Tejo; make sure you request these when making a reservation. A rooftop bar (also open to non-residents) serves light meals, and the terrace is the perfect place to enjoy a romantic breakfast. The pace is slow, atmosphere peaceful and ideally suited to couples; the busy city centre feels a million miles away. Not an ideal choice for those who like to be in the thick of the action. There are certainly more luxurious hotels in Lisbon, but few that possess the same captivating charm.

Style 7, Atmosphere 8, Location 7

As Janelas Verdes, Rua das Janelas Verdes 47, Lapa.
Tel: 21 396 8143 www.heritage.pt
Rates: €155–245

This former 18th-century palace was once the home of Portuguese novelist Eça de Queiros and supposedly the inspiration for his novels *O Ramalhete* and *Os Maias*. In turn, his one-time presence can be felt in the many *objets d'art*, books, paintings and mementos that fill this small and intimate hotel. All 29 rooms are bright and cheerful, some with virtually uninterrupted views of the Tejo. A communal library with a terrace is a wonderful spot for relaxing, and taking stock of the day ahead; it's particularly pleasant at about 5pm when the late afternoon sun sweeps through the building. Combined with the honesty bar next door (a Hoteis Heritage trait), it's incentive enough never to leave. A winding cast-iron staircase leads to a patio garden where breakfast is served daily. Despite being within walking-distance of the Santos and Docas nightlife, the hotel's elevated position guarantees peace and quiet. Guests are of the cultured and respectable type and elderly couples celebrating their golden wedding tend to predominate.

Style 8, Atmosphere 8, Location 8

● **Avenida Palace, Rua 1 de Dezembro 123, Baixa.**
Tel: 21 321 8100 www.hotel-avenida-palace.pt
Rates: €135–200

With a central location and luxurious premises, the Hotel Avenida Palace has a captive audience – and the owners sure know it! Originally built in 1892, this historic building underwent a $7 million renovation in 1998. Local designers Lucien Donnat and João Chichorro used a blend of Louis XV, Louis XVI, Dona Maria, Dom José and classic Imperial styles to decorate the interior. The result is a clumsy mish-mash of furnishings that conflict rather than contrast – all at the expense of good taste. In its defence, the hotel enjoys a sense of grandeur and character unrivalled in this part of town. Vast ballrooms complete with chandeliers, along with long marble corridors, hint at opulent bygone eras. Marble bathrooms are cavernous and all rooms soundproofed. But make sure you look the part; hostile staff are unnecessarily snooty and stirred only by the colour of money. The hotel is conveniently located next to Rossio station.

Style 6, Atmosphere 6, Location 9

Carlton Pestana Palace, Rua Jau 54, Santa Amaro.
Tel: 21 361 5600 www.pestana.com
Rates: €240–2,400

Currently regarded as the best hotel in Lisbon, this former 19th-century palace of the Marquis de Valle Flor is classified as a national monument. The four suites and communal areas within the former palace took almost 10 years to restore, with stained-glass windows specially sent from the Vatican. Original features remain in these rooms, with antique furnishings collected from across the globe. The only hotel in Portugal with a chapel, the

Pestana is currently awaiting permission from the archbishop to hold wedding ceremonies. The new palace extension comprises 192 rooms, divided into 'sunrise' and 'sunset' wings. The landscaped botanical gardens are a source of calm and serenity, and contain many flowers unique to Portugal. A marble swimming pool lies on the site of a former lake and a Chinese pavilion offers light meals in the summer. Guests also benefit from a modern health club and the highly respected Valle Flor restaurant. A relatively remote location proves to be the only downside to this unique hotel. Modern luxury with historical character.

Style 9, Atmosphere 9, Location 7

Dom Pedro Hotel Lisboa, Avenida Eng Duarte Pacheco 24.
Tel: 21 389 6600 www.dompedro.com
Rates: €185–400

This five-star high-rise is part of an Italian/Portuguese chain and caters mainly for business customers. Towering above the Amoreiras shopping mall and a busy dual carriageway, it's not exactly pedestrian-friendly and is probably best reached by car. That said, all 263 rooms are extremely comfortable and the amenities good. The corner suites on higher floors command fantastic views of the city, with wall-to-wall windows on all sides. Guests staying in the tower rooms have access to a VIP lounge and limited fitness facilities, and massages are also available. The opulent, mock 18th-century décor is at times stomach-churning, but at least distracts from a legion of suits armed with laptops. Great if you're looking for a city centre hotel slightly off the main drag, and the outdoor restaurant terrace is perfect for a summer's evening.

Style 7, Atmosphere 6, Location 7

Fenix Lisboa, Praca Marquês de Pombal 8, Avenida.
Tel: 21 386 2121 www.fenixlisboa.com
Rates: € 150–360

Directly overlooking the Marquês de Pombal roundabout, the Fenix Lisboa is largely indistinguishable from the plethora of multi-storey hotels in this busy district. However, the Brazilian Fenix chain has invested several million in a two-year renovation project which they hope will raise the hotel into the up-market bracket. Portuguese architect Massa Pina has worked wonders with the space; communal areas use a colour scheme of sobering grey with hints of oriental green and pink. It's a relaxed environment that's easy on the eye. Rooms are simple and straightforward, with all the obvious mod-cons. The hotel is geared mainly towards business clients attending conferences on the premises. It is easily reached by road and metro, and is within walking-distance of the city's top boutiques. A respectable all-rounder.

● **Four Seasons Hotel Ritz, Rua Rodrigo da Fonseca 88, Rato.**
Tel: 21 381 1400 www.fourseasons.com/lisbon
Rates: €305–460

Originally the vision of Portuguese dictator Oliveira Salazar, this luxurious five-star hotel was built with the intention of promoting Lisbon as both a centre of culture and high-class tourism. With no expense spared, more than 40,000sq.m of rare marble was used to fill the modernist structure, which was finally completed in 1959. Notable local artists were invited to contribute sculptures, paintings and tapestries as a legacy of contemporary arts. Following a post-revolutionary fallow period, the Four Seasons chain took over ownership in 1997. The original director's daughter still has heavy input in the design of the building and much of its character remains unsullied. The 10-storey building is set atop a hill, apart from the busy main drag and all 282 rooms command unparalleled views of the old city, Tejo river and Eduardo VII park (and all but 10 have private balconies). Other notable features include the well-respected Varanda restaurant and a new *feng shui*-inspired spa – easily the best in Lisbon. Access to the fantastic facilities is restricted to guests and exclusive members. Luxury on a large scale for those who like to stay centrally.

Style 9, Atmosphere 7, Location 8

Hotel Altis, Rua Castilho 11, Rato.
Tel: 21 310 6060 www.hotel-altis.pt
Rates: €180–450

Primarily a hotel for business customers, the Altis suffers from a drab and stale atmosphere. That said, this 303-room, city-centre hotel offers a generous range of facilities. The heated indoor swimming pool is somewhat larger than the usual toe-dippers and the gym is well equipped. The Rendez Vous coffee shop,

serving light meals all day, is a welcome addition and gives this otherwise slightly sterile establishment a sense of vibrancy. The roof top, with original 1970s leather seating, is a popular choice for businessmen and politicians. The Altis also offers self-contained apartments in a block over the road, suitable for longer stays. Complete with kitchenette, living area and study space, they benefit from a greater degree of privacy. Comfortable, convenient and functional.

Style 6, Atmosphere 6, Location 7

● **Hotel Britania, Rua Rodrigues Sampaio 17, Avenida.**
Tel: 21 315 5016 www.heritage.pt
Rates: €165–230

Marlene Dietrich could have sauntered her way to Hollywood and back on the marble floors of this 1940s masterpiece. Designed by the famous Portuguese architect Cassiano Branco, much of this grand hotel has been restored to its former glory. Art Deco light fittings dominate the hallways, while works of modern art line the walls. A barber's room from the original

hotel remains as an exhibition piece and hints at the exclusive gentlemen's set who once frequented this place. The 24-hour self-service bar is a buzz of civilized activity, played out on a hand-crafted floor made with woods from Portugal's ex-colonies. But Britania is not a museum piece. As is characteristic of this small hotel chain, guests are invited to feel at home. Rooms are spacious, with subtle lighting, and contain all the original furniture (although we're assured mattresses have been changed!). Set back on a street parallel to the busy Avenida da Liberdade, Britania enjoys both relative quiet and a central location. Remember to pack a twin-set or smoking jacket in your suit-case, and feel like a million dollars.

Style 9, Atmosphere 7, Location 7

Hotel Lisboa Plaza, Trav. Salitre/Av. Liberdade, Avenida.
Tel: 21 321 8218 www.heritage.pt
Rates: €165–380

Housing 94 rooms, this is the largest and newest of the hotels in the Hoteis Heritage family, but a warm and friendly service ensures there is no compromise on the homely atmosphere. The décor is courtesy of Portuguese interior designer Graça Viterbo and is colonial but relaxed. Rooms are heavily laden with uphol-stery and suffer a lack of natural light, but command pleasant

views over the botanical gardens and Lisbon's one-time theatrical district. Suites are spacious, with a study and lounge area. An adjoining door is also provided for families who want their children to stay in a twin room next to them. A banquet-style buffet lunch attracts a hungry horde of non-residents and claims many a victim whose eyes are bigger than their stomach. It's a real bargain at €24 a head: even a Roman emperor would have trouble munching his way through this lot.

Style 7, Atmosphere 7, Location 7

Hotel Metrópole, Praça Dom Pedro IV Rossio 30, Baixa.
Tel: 21 321 9030 www.almeidahotels.com
Rates: €112–124

This Art Nouveau building occupies the space above Café Nicola, in the heart of Rossio. The impressive white façade masks an interior in need of some modernization. Nevertheless, rooms are clean and spacious; some include original 1920s furnishings, and the marble-decorated bathrooms are relatively luxurious. Several of the rooms have balconies, with views of the São Jorge castle and Rossio square. The building also has a poignant history: communist revolutionaries addressed the city from these very windows during the 1974 revolution. Now it's just a great spot to watch Lisbon go about its business. The hotel bar is pleasant, but older guests intent on sightseeing rarely stop for long. By day rooms can be noisy: that's the price for being in the thick of the action. Restaurants, bars, cafés and major attractions are within easy walking distance and a constant stream of taxis

will ferry guests further afield.

Style 5, Atmosphere 6, Location 9

Hotel Real Palácio, Rua Tomas Ribeiro 115, Saldanha.
Tel: 21 319 9500 www.hoteisreal.com
Rates: €150–360

It may lack the grandeur of the Carlton Pestana, but this recently rebuilt 18th-century palace offers grand surroundings in a central location. Portuguese interior designer Graça Viterbo, also responsible for the Lisboa Plaza, has tastefully emulated a subtle regal design using his trademark pastel colour scheme. There are 147 rooms in total, 12 of which are housed within the former

palace walls. These overlook an interior courtyard, where musical events occasionally take place. The standard rooms are both light and airy, and a third of them have balconies. You can take dinner on an outdoor terrace, which provides a pleasant mixture of vibrant colour and satisfying angles. A small but newly refurbished health club is an equally welcome addition. More up-market than its sister hotel, Real Park, the Palácio is a refreshing alternative to the grotesquely ornate and outmoded establishments which seem to dominate the city centre.

Style 8, Atmosphere 7, Location 7

Hotel Venezia, Avenida da Liberdade 189, Avenida.
Tel: 21 352 2618 www.3khoteis.com
Rates: €75–130

A wonderfully ornate spiral staircase dominates this small hotel in the heart of Lisbon's hotel district. A decorative stained-glass skylight scatters shards of light onto the salmon-pink walls lined

with chandeliers. Originally built as a palace in 1886, the hotel is a listed building and many features remain intact. The only new addition is a mural of Lisbon which fills the entrance. Unfortunately, for security reasons, guests are no longer able to use the stairwell and have to make do with a stuffy matchbox lift instead. Rooms are pleasant, although the matching curtains and bedspread combination can be a little overwhelming, and carpets branded with the grotesque company insignia can make you feel as if you're sleeping in a cereal packet. Attic rooms on the third floor all have sloping ceilings and can only be described as 'cosy' (and probably best avoided if you're over 5ft 3in). Parking is available at the rear of the building. Despite a charming and picturesque shell, style-wise, Venezia is lacking in ssubstance. A unique building, nonetheless.

Style 6, Atmosphere 6, Location 6

Lapa Palace, Rua do Pau da Bandeira 4, Lapa.
Tel: 21 394 9494 www.orient-expresshotels.com
Rates: €325–2,400

Owned by the Orient Express group, this breathtaking residence
easily deserves its first-class reputation. Set in tropical gardens
with towering ficus trees, waterfalls and a heated swimming pool,
the 19th-century palace was once home to the Count of
Valencia. Now a listed building, all architectural extensions have
been made according to a strict set of guidelines. The interior
consists of brightly polished marble floors, floral drapes and aristocratic furnishings. Rooms range from pleasing to the truly magnificent, each with a balcony or terrace. Famous actors and rock
stars opt for rooms on the 7th floor, where each has been

designed according to a different theme. If you're feeling really
flush, ask for room 701, which has its very own turret where you
can have a champagne breakfast. Service is charming and always
attentive. Fine Italian cuisine is served at the Cipriani restaurant
and the generous buffet breakfast is not to be missed. A range of
aromatherapy and beauty therapies is available, all using La
Prairie products. A trained MAC make-up artist can also be
booked for appointments. The hotel enjoys a quiet location and
very little passing traffic, although this does mean guests rely
heavily on the hotel's over-inflated taxi service. But that's a small
price to pay when you're in the Lapa luxury.

Lisboa Regency Chiado, Rua Nova do Almada 114, Baixa.
Tel: 21 325 6100 www.regency-hotels-resorts.com
Rates: €144–345

In terms of location and style, this city-centre design hotel blows all competition out of the water. It can be reached via an entrance at the bottom of fashionable Rua Garrett and shares a

building with the neighbouring shopping centre. Designed by the same architect who was also responsible for the Carlton Pestana Palace, the décor is inspired by the Orient, with a flush of warm and tranquil colours; nothing is overstated. Rooms are remarkably bright and instantly relaxing; those on the 7th floor also have a private veranda overlooking the Baixa. Specially selected flowers, chosen to reflect the hotel's colour scheme, blossom on the rooftop. Embroidered silk cushions are scattered throughout the bar and an elegant rectangular window extends into the upstairs restaurant, flooding the building with light. Unsurprisingly, the hotel is popular with a style-savvy and trendsetting elite.

Style 9, Atmosphere 8, Location 9

Lisboa Tejo Hotel, Rua dos Condes de Monsanto 2, Baixa.
Tel: 21 886 6182 www.hotellisboatejo.com
Rates: €80–100

This recently renovated design hotel lies in the heart of Baixa behind the main city squares, and is ideal for a short break. City shops, cafés and restaurants are within split-second distance. The Phillippe Starck style/modern European interior is a mixture of *azzurro* blues and quirky fixtures: guests are greeted with a tumbling stone waterfall, while fresh apples fill shelf-space behind the reception desk. The ancient Arabic Borratem Well, which once supplied all of Lisbon, falls within the hotel walls and has been carefully preserved. Although space is at a premium, rooms are warm and homely. However, they do cross a fine line between style innovation and MFI bedroom. There are plenty more impressive hotels in Lisbon, but many would struggle to achieve such all-round quality.

Style 8, Atmosphere 8, Location 9

Le Meridien Park Atlantic, Rua Castilho 149, Rato.
Tel: 21 381 8700 www.lemeridien-lisbon.com
Rates: €260–375

Part of the French hotel group, this 331-room hotel can be found at the Marquês de Pombal roundabout overlooking the landscaped Eduardo VII park. It's a popular destination for large tour groups, but recent renovations have elevated the modern premises beyond hotel chain status. New rooms enjoy a *feng shui*-inspired décor and Philippe Starck-styled bathrooms; it's a look to rival the handful of design hotels in the city. Clients who opt for the top suite are also able to invite guests for a soirée on their private balcony. The service and facilities are equally impressive: on-site cinema screenings are frequently arranged and guests are entitled to discount rates at the Clube VII health and sports complex opposite. The company has also invested in the hotel's bars and restaurants as separate entities; the L'Appart brasserie is laid out as different rooms of a house and the Ganesh bar is a jumble of Eastern influences. Surprisingly stylish for a chain hotel.

Style 8, Atmosphere 8, Location 7

NH Liberdade, Avenida da Liberdade 180, Avenida.
Tel: 21 351 4060 www.nh-hotels.com
Rates: €230–335

Part of the rapidly expanding Spanish chain, this stylish and modern hotel is popular with both business clients and design-conscious tourists. The matt black *feng shui*-inspired interior is a mixture of eye-pleasing angles and tasteful order. Rooms are more like mini-apartments, with basic kitchen and coffee-making facilities. And with complimentary video game consoles and pay-to-view films, it's surprising anyone actually steps outside! If the lure of creature comforts does prove too strong, don't worry:

specially commissioned photographs of Lisbon feature as a permanent exhibition in every room. The bedroom colour schemes vary, depending on how much light they receive. Such attention to detail is both admirable and rare for a hotel chain of this size. Guests are offered a 'pillow menu' on arrival, along with an extremely generous selection of bathroom toiletries. A roof-top terrace commands fantastic views of the city and cocktail parties can be arranged for groups on request. NH is one of the few hotels in Lisbon with a swimming pool. But if you're training for the Olympics, forget it – it's strictly for lounging.

Style 9, Atmosphere 7, Location 8

Olissipo, Rua Costa do Castelo 112, Graça.
Tel: 21 882 0190
Rates: €98–120

The Olissipo is a relatively large and modern hotel for an area characterized by crumbling guesthouses. Situated within one of the most tranquil districts of Lisbon, it's the perfect choice for couples in search of a romantic break. The winding backstreets of historical Alfama are within walking distance and the choice of fantastic *miradouros* is endless. The hotel itself boasts all sorts of modern facilities and staff are friendly and welcoming. A generous but limited parking area is available, although guests are unable to book in advance. Rooms are inoffensive, but mottled wallpaper and plaster fittings resemble a suburban show home. Still, the spacious private terraces enjoyed by the rooms on the second and third floors are a nice touch. The bulk of guests are early-to-bed, early-to-rise middle-class tourists. Definitely not the place for a party, but ideal for those who crave peace and quiet.

Style 7, Atmosphere 6, Location 7

Palácio Belmonte, Pateo Dom Fradique 14, Alfama.
Tel: 21 881 6600 www.palaciobelmonte.com
Rates: €300–1,200

Possibly the most interesting residence in Lisbon, and easily the most expensive. Built in 1449, the palace survived the devastating 1755 earthquake and remained in the Belmonte family for over five centuries. Sadly the property fell into disrepair and the final occupants, two old ladies, were restricted to living in one of the towers. Four years ago Frederic P. Coustols, the French architectural philanthropist, stepped in to restore the building. Regarded by many as a genius, this eccentric collector of houses had already purchased and rebuilt a village in southern France. All eight rooms of the palace were restored using traditional Portuguese techniques. The project is also an experiment in ecology: a natural ventilation system has been used in place of electrical air-conditioning and even materials used to clean the complex are biodegradable. The result is breathtaking and a work of art, not to mention architectural mastery. Coustols has combined painstaking attention to detail with his own irreverent style of interior design: fantastical Tim Burton-esque candelabras jut out from walls covered in 38,000 carefully restored *azulejos*. Definitely worth a visit, even if you can't afford a stay. A dream property, with an otherworldly price tag to match.

Style 9/10, Atmosphere 9, Location 8

Quinta Nova da Conceição, Rua Cidade de Rabat 5.
Tel: 21 778 0091
Rates: €140

A former residence of the Count of Benfica, this 18th-century country house is Lisbon's only Turismo de Habitação, a government-monitored scheme that allows tourists to stay in anything from a cottage to a castle as a guest of the owner. Only three of the 52 rooms, all with private bathrooms, are available to book. Communal areas include an *azulejo*-tiled breakfast room, a grand living area, and an exotic wood-crafted library where numerous secret political liaisons have allegedly taken place. Situated within half a hectare of land, an outdoor swimming pool and tennis courts are also available. Current owner Teresa welcomes guests to treat the palace as their own, as long as they are prepared to live with her dogs! Furniture originates from various periods and some exquisite pieces can be found throughout the house. Teresa has little clue as to their worth and is keen to treat the building as a living entity rather than a museum-piece. Her rather eccentric taste in interior design is certainly heart-warming; don't be surprised to find a cabbage-shaped candle atop

a mahogany grand piano. Since the hotel is located north of the city, the surroundings are remarkably unimpressive – a mixture of motorway intersections and sprawling suburbs. However, the close proximity of Benfica stadium means that guests can hear a goal from the comfort of their own palace.

Style 9, Atmosphere 9, Location 5

Sheraton Lisboa, Rua Latinho Coelho 1, Saldanha.
Tel: 21 312 0000 www.starwood.com/sheraton
Rates: €130–240

A defining point on Lisbon's undulating skyline, this gleaming multi-storey is the tallest high-rise in the city. Owned by the

Starwood group (also responsible for the W chain of US design hotels), the Sheraton smacks overwhelmingly of international travel. Wealthy businessmen and conference attendees flit constantly about the beige marble lobby. Rooms are pleasantly decorated, but are impressively functional rather than comfortably relaxing. At times the suit-to-trainer ratio is over 4:1 and the building starts to resemble an office block in both appearance and pace. Reception staff have a tendency to look down their noses at guests who don't dress the part. A top-floor restaurant offers a panoramic view, but is not recommended to those who suffer from vertigo or a fear of lifts. The hotel can be found in the Saldanha business district. Reliable quality.

Style 7, Atmosphere 7, Location 6

Solar do Castelo, Rua das Cozinhas 2, Graça.
Tel: 21 887 0909 www.heritage.pt
Rates: €182–280

The latest addition to the family-run Hoteis Heritage Lisboa group, this unique residence enjoys an excellent location in the peaceful grounds of the Castelo de São Jorge. A former 18th-century mansion, it still retains some of the characteristic Pombaline architectural features. The emphasis is very much on hospitality, and guests are invited to treat the voluptuous lounge area as their own. A self-service bar and open-plan courtyard

add to the atmosphere of relaxed intimacy. Several of the suites open onto the mustard-coloured terrace, bathed in changing light from Lisbon's glorious sunsets. Others offer a fantastic view of the castle walls. Breakfast is served between 7.30 and 11.30, but an eager-to-please kitchen staff are happy to rustle something up later in the day – so lie-ins are still an option. And if you get peckish, don't worry; china urns filled with tangerines are available for guests to nibble at. It's removed from the centre of town, but this hotel boasts a quality of design surprisingly rare in Lisbon. There are only 14 rooms available, so reservations are strongly recommended.

Style 9, Atmosphere 9, Location 8

Solar dos Mouros, Rua do Milagre de Santo Antonio 6.
Tel: 21 885 4940 www.solardosmouros.pt
Rates: €106–190

The concept behind this 11-room residence runs in much the same vein as nearby Palácio Belmonte: each space has its own distinct character, with an overall emphasis on intimacy. This is another Lisbon hotel owned by a Frenchman – artist and collector Luis Lemos – but is far less extravagant and expensive than the Belmonte. Contemporary works of art, including several by Lemos himself, have been carefully selected to give each area individual character. The spacious rooms are more like mini apartments, with sofas and stereo equipment. Staff are also happy to accommodate three people to a room – an ideal option for friends. Built within the foundations of the Porto d'Alfofa, which once gave access to the Castle, the hotel combines hilltop views of the city with the convenience of a mere 5-minute walk to the town centre. Communal areas are thin on the ground, although a guest bar is due to open this year. Prices are exceptionally reasonable for a hotel of this quality.

Style 9, Atmosphere 8, Location 8

● **Tivoli Jardim, Rua Julio Caesar Machado 7–9, Avenida.**
Tel: 21 359 1000 www.tivolihotels.com
Rates: €114–185

Located behind the five-star Tivoli Lisboa, this sister hotel offers simpler surroundings at a cheaper rate. Set back from the busy Avenida, the mood is considerably less hectic than other hotels in the area. An unsightly car park obscures the entrance, but noise is never a problem. Admittedly the rooms are disappointingly mediocre – think four-star motorway motel – but all modern facilities are provided. The hotel's key redeeming feature is a large outdoor swimming pool and sheltered garden space shared with the Tivoli Lisboa. It's a great place to soak up some sun in between serious shopping trips. Thankfully the Jardim seems to have escaped the coach-loads of tour groups who descend on its sister premises. Instead, quiet couples and small groups drift through the remarkably pleasant but underused bar area.

Style 6, Atmosphere 6, Location 8

● **Tivoli Lisboa, Avenida da Liberdade 185, Avenida.**
Tel: 21 319 8900 www.tivolihotels.com
Rates: €170–630

The flagship hotel in Portugal's prestigious Tivoli group, the Hotel Tivoli Lisboa first opened its revolving doors to customers in 1933. Complete with porters decked in tails and top hats, it wouldn't look out of place in London's Park Lane. An expansive lobby filled with scatter cushions and boutique shopping bags is permanently a hub of activity and at times resembles an airport waiting lounge. The hotel rooftop grill restaurant is worth a visit

– if only for the incredible view! Rooms are highly decorated – in fact, may be painfully opulent for ordinary tastes. The most attractive facility on offer is an outdoor swimming pool shared with the neighbouring Tivoli Jardim, secluded within a beautiful garden; refreshments are served at the poolside. Given a convenient location halfway along the Avenida da Liberdade and a five-star rating, the hotel attracts a wide range of clients: businessmen, couples, families and coach-loads of tour groups. It may lack the intimacy of a smaller establishment, but the Tivoli Lisboa is a safe bet if comfort is the main concern.

Style 7, Atmosphere 7, Location 8

Vila Galé Opera, Travessa Conde da Ponte, Alcântara.
Tel: 21 360 5400 www.vilagale.pt
Rates: €90–147

This ultra-modern hotel takes its name from the neighbouring classical music schools and the musical theme is conspicuous throughout the building: each floor is named after a different genre and each room an artist. Theatre groups and singers also perform regularly in the Portuguese/French restaurant. It's a nice idea, but the emphasis on music is both baffling and over-egged; lifesize mannequins of famous opera characters hang pointlessly behind a glass cabinet at the end of an open-plan lobby. Needless to say, the po-faced staff appear equally inanimate. On the plus side, the hotel benefits from a well-equipped health club with

personal trainers at the ready to assist less motivated fitness freaks. The Opera can be found on the road to Belém, and is a welcome alternative to the many city centre hotels. Several rooms also enjoy fantastic views of the suspension bridge. Business groups and moneyed young professionals make up the bulk of guests.

Style 8, Atmosphere 7, Location 7

VIP Eden, Praça dos Restauradores 24, Baixa.
Tel: 21 321 6600
Rates: €89–180

Regarded by some as a grand statement and others as a grotesque monstrosity, this controversial hotel is hard to miss. The space formerly belonged to the Eden cinema and much of the Art Deco façade has been restored. The effect is marred only by tacky plastic palm trees that dominate the building and are totally incongruous; it's less of an oasis and more of an eyesore. However, a central location and self-contained apartment facilities make this a popular choice with businessmen and longer-stay travellers. There are 75 studios (suitable for two people) and 59 apartments (sleeping up to four people), all with kitchen and desk facilities. A rooftop swimming pool and bar are appealing features in summer months. Rooms are clean and thankfully less ostentatious than the hotel exterior. A good choice for groups travelling on a budget.

Style 6, Atmosphere 7, Location 9

York House, Rua das Janelas Verdes 32, Lapa.
Tel: 21 396 2435 www.yorkhouselisboa.com
Rates: €140–260

A former Carmelite convent, this delightful guesthouse continues to enjoy both privacy and sanctity. Located in the sleepy Lapa district, the hotel is reached via a pink-walled staircase which opens out onto a terrace filled with bright flowers, plants and trailing vines. It's easy to see why such writers as Graham Greene and John Le Carré chose to stay here on their visits to

Lisbon. There are 36 rooms housed within the 17th-century building, complete with solid wood furnishings and four-poster beds. Despite the many decorative references to the hotel's religious past, this laid-back residence is anything but austere and feels more like a country retreat. The hotel acquired its name after two Yorkshire ladies rented the property in 1880 and turned it into a guesthouse. The Portuguese restaurant comes highly recommended and during the summer months food is served on the leafy terrace; it's one of the few quality outdoor eating spots in the city! Rooms are quickly snapped up, so it's best to book in advance.

Style 8, Atmosphere 9, Location 8

eat...

No visitor will leave hungry on a trip to Lisbon. The city boasts an impressive range of restaurants, all of a competitively high quality. From bastions of traditional Portuguese cuisine (Tasquina da Adelaide, Solar dos Nunes) to international hotspots (sushi bar Aya, pizza palace Casa Nova), there are tastes to suit most palates. Unless, of course, you're vegetarian, in which case a weekend of bread and boiled vegetables awaits you!

The Portuguese love to eat and food is very much steeped in their social culture. No Lisboeta would even contemplate a night out without first lining their stomach. Consequently, Friday and Saturday nights are a restaurant roadblock and booking is essential. As you'll quickly realize, everything happens late in Lisbon; most parties will not arrive for dinner until 10 or 11pm. For an upbeat, party atmosphere, head to the Bairro Alto area where a cluster of good restaurants can be found; Oliviers and Sinal Vermelho come highly recommended. During the week locals choose to stay indoors and most restaurants close on either a Sunday or Monday.

Portuguese cooking is traditionally heavy; a meat and carbohydrate culture continues to prevail. Portions are large, so expect to loosen your trouser belt a notch or two. If in doubt, opt for a *meia doce* (half portion). Often a selection of olives, cheese, meats and bread will be brought to the table – even if not requested. You'll be charged for whatever you eat. Dishes of fish (grilled, fried, boiled or oven-baked) or game are served with vegetables and potatoes. Much originates from the Alentejo region (Portugal's bread basket). For authentic home-cooked food, head to 1 de Maio or Primavera.

One speciality difficult to ignore is the ubiquitous *bacalhau* (dried and salted codfish). There are supposedly 365 ways of cooking this national favourite – one for every day of the year. Other local delicacies include *acorda* (a bread-based pudding resembling porridge) and *feijoada* (a bean stew with the odd pig's ear thown in); to taste-test both, try Pap' Açorda and Mercado de Santa Clara, respectively. Lisbon's proximity to the sea makes seafood a popular option. Head to one of the city's many *cervejerias* (beer halls) for a shellfish feast in informal surroundings. Try Ramiro for reliable quality or Gambrinus for a fine dining experience.

Wine remains the drink of choice in Portugal. Lists can be exhaustive and confusing. Generally whites are better than reds and the Douro, Bairrada, Ribatejo and Oeste regions are a safe bet. *Vinho verde* ('green wine') from Minho in the north is a sparkling, spiky wine best enjoyed in summer months. Portugal is also famous for its port production, most notably in the Douro region.

Eating in Lisbon is always an all-round experience, so expect to meet some interesting characters on your culinary travels; Sua Excelência and Bolshoi make for unique entertainment. Despite its size, the city uses its space in a particularly impressive way. Restaurants in remarkable settings include A Travessa (a former convent), Enoteca (an ancient aqueduct), Estufa Real (a royal greenhouse) and Kais (a tram warehouse).

All the restaurants in this section have been rated according to food, service and atmosphere. The prices given are for three courses for one, with half a bottle of wine.

Our top ten restaurants in Lisbon are:
1. A Travessa
2. Gambrinus
3. XL
4. Oliviers
5. Bico do Sapato
6. Sua Excelência
7. Chapitô
8. Kais
9. Os Corvos
10. Galeria

Our top five restaurants for food are:
1. A Travessa
2. Gambrinus
3. Oliviers
4. Tasquina da Adelaide
5. XL

Our top five restaurants for service are:
1. Gambrinus
2. Kais
3. Sua Excelência
4. Os Corvos
5. Bolshoi

Our top five restaurants for atmosphere are:
1. XL
2. A Travessa
3. Bico do Sapato
4. Chapitô
5. Bolshoi

1 de Maio, Rua da Atalaia 8, Bairro Alto.
Tel: 21 342 6840
Open: noon–3pm, 7–10.30pm.
Closed Saturday lunch and Sunday.   €25

Tables are consistently full at this traditional Bairro Alto *adega* (wine cellar), as it's a popular choice with both tourists and locals. An inconspicuous entrance on Rua da Atalaia would be easily missed if it were not for the queues of hungry hopefuls who gather outside nightly. The interior, a mixture of typical white-tiled walls and wooden tables illuminated by harsh 120 watt bulbs, is nothing to write home about. It's also not for the

claustrophobic: during busy times a trip to the loo can involve military planning. The food itself, mainly fish and meat dishes, is simple and delicious, and makes an ideal introduction to local cuisine. Staff speak little English, but the menu is fairly straightforward so you shouldn't go far wrong. Red-cheeked and rotund diners tend to fill the limited space, and conversation is a near-impossibility without bellowing. A well-priced, no-nonsense example of Portuguese cooking at its best, and a guaranteed crowd-pleaser.

Food 8, Service 8, Atmosphere 7

Alcântara Café, Rua Maria Luisa Holstein 15, Alcântara.
Tel: 21 363 7176
Open: 8pm–1am daily   €50

A pillar of fashion in its 1980s heyday, this converted docks warehouse continues to maintain its reputation, despite losing ground to newer and more exciting restaurants. Designed by Antonio Pinto, the décor is a mixture of dining-room decadence and industrial renovation. Yards of red velvet are draped across *faux-classique* steel pillars and soft lighting lends a warmth and intimacy to the open-plan space. The effect is surprisingly tasteful and not at all garish. The red-carpet treatment begins immediately: diners are greeted at the door and swept along a plush hallway to their tables. The atmosphere is electric. Staff tend to your every need and steer their tight ship with military precision. High-flying execs and showbiz stars frequent, although every customer commands celebrity status for the duration of their three courses. Owner of the restaurant, Portuguese entrepreneur and TV star Herman José, also presents his chat show from the premises regularly. Unfortunately Alcântara is a victim of all surface and no substance, and the food is disappointing for a restaurant of this calibre. But people don't come to Alcântara to eat: they come to be seen and to feel like they're worth seeing. The restaurant is busy at weekends and reservations are essential.

Food 6, Service 8, Atmosphere 8

A Picanha, Rua das Janelas Verdes 96, Lapa.

Tel: 21 397 5401 www.picanha-janelasverdes.com
Open: 12.30–3.30pm, 7.30–midnight.
Closed Saturday and Sunday lunch.   €19

A carnivore's heaven, a vegetarian's hell; there is only one thing
on the menu at Picanha and that's meat. A Brazillian speciality,
picanha is a method of barbecuing rump steak with garlic.
Succulent shavings are carved up and piled high on plates, with
only refried beans and a salad selection as an accompaniment. In
fact, the only say you have is how cooked you like your cow. The
all-you-can-eat set menu (well, it makes the decision process
straightforward) is a bargain even by continental standards and
will set you well on the way to that first colonic irrigation. The
restaurant itself is small and the *azulejo*-covered walls elevate
what is essentially a beefed-up canteen to a higher level. Waiting
staff are young and the mood lively – particularly after a couple
of *caipirinhas*! Not the place to take a first date or a Tibetan
monk.

Food 8, Service 7, Atmosphere 7

A Travessa, Travessa das Inglesinhas 28, Lapa.

Tel: 21 390 2034
Open: 12.30–3.30pm, 8pm–midnight.
Closed Saturday lunch and Sunday.   €50

Mention Travessa to any Lisboeta and they'll probably smile fondly as if recalling a close friend or a first love. That's because in the last 25 years this Belgian restaurant has achieved an identity way beyond a room full of tables and chairs. In fact, its popularity has necessitated a move to the current spacious premises: a former 17th-century convent in the sleepy backstreets of Lapa. Whatever the weather, the welcome is always warm: during the summer up to 100 tables are set up in the open-air courtyard and in winter guests are treated to a log fire. During the week a menu of international food is served, dependent on changes in season and market. The emphasis is mainly on fresh fish and meat, with melt-in-the-mouth slow roasted pork as an unrivalled speciality. Fresh bread is baked daily on the premises in a stone oven and owner Antonio regularly offers loaves to the late-night revellers. On Saturday night, mussels are the only order of the day and reservations essential. Neither ultra-trendy nor over-hyped, Travessa is one of those restaurants that both meets and exceeds all expectations.

Food 9, Service 9, Atmosphere 9/10

Aya, Twin Towers, Rua Campolide 56, Loja.
Tel: 21 727 1155
Open: 12.30–2.30pm, 7.30–10pm daily.   €35

Few tourists would come to Portugal in search of a Japanese restaurant, but Aya exemplifies the high quality of international cuisine to be found in Lisbon. Initially a small Japanese restaurant in Lapa, this second opening at the Twin Towers shopping arcade has proved far more popular with locals. In contrast to the offerings of the numerous fashion-fad sushi bars springing up around the city, the menu is a mixture of traditional sushi, *sashimi* and *tempura*. About as authentic as it gets this side of the equator. Watching the immaculately attired chefs prepare dishes with mathematical precision is an experience in itself. On the downside, the language barrier is practically insurmountable. The unfortunate task of translating a Portuguese menu of Japanese dishes into English is more than taxing and should only be attempted by those with a grasp of either language or a lucky streak. Despite being part of a shopping and cinema complex,

Aya is more than just a food-hall fodder stop, but an out-of-town location means it is best reached by taxi. Not a conventional choice, but a godsend when the sight of more *bacalau* promises to send you sideways.

Food 9, Service 7, Atmosphere 7

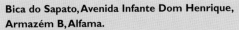

Bica do Sapato, Avenida Infante Dom Henrique, Armazém B, Alfama.
Tel: 21 881 0320 www.bicadosapato.com
Open: 12.30–2.30pm, 8–11.30pm. Closed Sunday.   €50

The pulse in Lisbon's trendiest esplanade development, this warehouse conversion found fame by virtue of its Hollywood

owner, actor John Malkovich. Now the restaurant stands alone as the slickest spot to dine in the city. Views of the Rio Tejo are stunning by day and electrifying by night. The vibrant and modern interior is lifted straight from a spread in *Wallpaper* and provides a fitting backdrop for the cutting-edge jet-set who arrive in packs. Sophisticated business lunches are the order of the day, while night-time revellers prefer to let their hair down – Saturday nights are particularly raucous. The pace really picks up when the restaurant closes, and party-goers move into the adjoining café area. Literally translated, '*bica do sapato*' means 'point of shoe' and you'll see plenty on the feet of beautiful *fashionistas*, enjoying a few cocktails before heading to hip club Lux (see page 156) next door. Despite recent claims to the contrary, the quality of food continues to be of a good standard and is a mix of seafood and modern European. Friendly chef Fernando was one-time owner of the popular Pap' Açorda in Bairro Alto. Beautiful food for beautiful people.

Food 9, Service 7, Atmosphere 9

Bolshoi, Rua Cruz dos Poiais 95-A, Bairro Alto.
Tel: 21 390 8480
Open: 8pm–1am. Closed Sunday.   €25

'Quirky' doesn't even come close to describing this bizarre backstreet Russian restaurant. Owner Elena Hallin, a singer and multilinguist, came to Lisbon with the intention of opening a dining house to celebrate her culture and bring happiness into people's lives. It's an aim she's certainly achieved. Bolshoi already has a cult following among young trendsetters, who regularly queue for a seat that was most likely rescued from a rubbish tip. A sequin-laden Elena greets guests individually and invites them to

leave their troubles at the door. The menu arrives on a torn piece of brown paper bag and generally consists of whatever the kitchen still has knocking about. But people don't come to Bolshoi for the food. When the mood suits her Elena takes to her synthesizer and entertains guests with a rendition of Russian songs. Her diva-like outfit changes are always meet with rapturous applause. It's vaudeville entertainment of the highest quality. If you're after a night to remember, there's no better choice.

Food 5, Service 9, Atmosphere 9

Casa Nostra, Travessa Poço da Cidade 60, Bairro Alto.
Tel: 21 342 5931
Open: 12.30–2.30pm, 8–11pm.
Closed Saturday lunch and Monday.   €40

Now in its 20th year, this Bairro Alto classic is still the best Italian eatery in Lisbon. The menu is small but of a consistently high standard, and offers interesting and mouth-watering

variations on the usual Italian standards of pizza and pasta. Italian chef Maria Paola already commands a near-devotional following among diners. Windows in the front room open out onto the street, offering a breath of fresh air by day and irresistible people-watching by night. Designed by architect Manuel Graça Dias, the refreshing mint-green interior is almost as delicious as the pesto dishes on the menu. The crowd is varied, but all share a common interest in good food and good taste. Intimate seating and crisply laid tables make for a homely but comfortably elegant atmosphere. Turn up without a reservation and you may have to wait for a while. But friendly staff will do their best to accommodate and may even offer you a complimentary drink while you wait!

Food 9, Atmosphere 8, Service 8

Casanova, Cais da Pedra a Bica do Sapato, Loja 7, Santa Apolónia.
Tel: 21 887 7532
Open: 12.30pm–2am Wednesday–Sunday; 6pm–2am Tuesday.
Closed Monday. €25

Opened by the Casa Nostra team three years ago, this bustling pizzeria is cheaper and far more informal than its *fratello grande*. Part of the trendy Santa Apolónia esplanade, the restaurant is a stone's throw from Bica do Sapato and attracts a younger and far more casual but nonetheless stylish crowd. The legendary melt-in-the-mouth pizza bases are otherworldly and better than most Neapolitan equivalents. Litres of wine are served by the carafe and food prices are reasonable, given the high quality. At weekends, families and young children swarm the outdoor terrace with its fantastic views of the Rio Tejo. No dinner reservations are taken and on Saturday nights queues can stretch for up to an hour. At times the smell of freshly baked dough, wafting from the wood-fired ovens, can be torturous. Arrive before 9pm if you can. Fast food that tastes great.

Food 9, Atmosphere 7, Service 7

Chapitô, Rua Costa do Castelo 7, Alfama.
Tel: 21 886 7334 www.chapito.org
Open: 7.30pm–midnight. Closed Monday.   €30

Part of the Chapitô community, this charming restaurant shares a spacious esplanade with the neighbouring circus school. It also shares the same bohemian and artistic ethos. A wooden spiral staircase leads to a dining area dotted with candlelight, and wall-to-wall windows offer easily the most captivating views of Lisbon. The effect is near fairy-tale and couples come here to gaze out to the illuminated suspension bridge and into each other's eyes. Fortunately, displays of affection are neither explicit

nor nauseating and big groups should not be put off. Indeed, early on in the evening the place is popular with young families. The set menu is divided into five colour co-ordinated sections, although dishes can be mixed and matched. Specials change weekly and are drawn from around the world. Service is friendly and always with a smile. Why not round off the evening with a theatre show or a drink in the Net Jazz Café (see page 116) below? An enchanting experience in magical surroundings.

Food 8, Service 9, Atmosphere 9

Charcuteria, Rua do Alecrim 47a, Chiado.
Tel: 21 342 3845
Open: 12.30–3pm, 7.30pm–12am.
Closed Saturday lunch and Sunday.   €43

The roots of this well-respected restaurant go back to 1949 when it opened as a small five-table *merceleria* in Campo de Ourique. It has since remained in the family and is currently in the hands of self-taught chef Manuel Martins. Charcuteria's reputation for solid but sophisticated Portuguese food quickly spread by word of mouth and necessitated a move to their current premises in Chiado. Dishes are inspired mainly by traditional recipes from the Alentejo, with fish and game featuring heavily. The emphasis is on flavour rather than fodder, and portions are smaller than the usual gargantuan amounts. An open-air terrace at the rear of the 18th-century Pombaline building is refreshingly pleasant on a summer's evening. Lanterns cascading shards of coloured light complete the romantic setting. By day, the restaurant attracts well-attired businessmen and wealthy it-girls who nibble and natter. Nights are usually reserved for couples.

Food 8, Service 7/8, Atmosphere 7/8

El Gordo, Travessa dos Fiéis de Deus 28, Bairro Alto.
Tel: 21 342 4266
Open: 5pm–2am daily   €45

There are two branches of this Spanish-style *tapas* bar, both within close proximity. The original premises is more spacious, whereas a newer restaurant in the heart of Bairro Alto enjoys outdoor seating and a larger slice of the nightlife action. The menu (a mix of vegetable, fish and meat dishes) is broad and can accommodate even the fussiest of eaters. It's the ideal choice for large groups who like to pick and mix their meals. But don't get too carried away: the bill quickly adds up and there have been complaints that prices are too steep. In spite of this tables are always full and you'll have to be quick to bag a space outdoors. The décor in both restaurants is elegantly bohemian and instantly comforting; delicate light spills from paper lanterns onto woven wall hangings, carved wooden screens and colourful glass tables. It's an Aladdin's den of knick-knacks and treasures. While

the restaurant is suitable for small groups and couples, the sister
premises will kick-start the night for greater gangs of revellers.

Food 7, Service 7, Atmosphere 8

Enoteca, Rua da Mãe d'Água a Praça da Alegria.
Tel: 21 342 2079
Open: 6pm–2am. Closed Monday.   €25

A wine bar in a former reservoir – a unique concept (by
Portuguese standards) in a unique space. An impressive selection
of both Portuguese and European fine wines is available by the
glass, along with a menu of accompanying cheese-based dishes.
Staff will gladly recommend complementary wines as well as
offering a fine wine tasting selection, which changes every fort-

night. Owner João Paulo Martins is Portugal's most famous wine writer, and you're likely to taste some of the best pressings the country has to offer. Dating back to 1781, the aqueduct forms part of the Grand Aqueduct in Praça Espanha. A tunnel, which can still be viewed, leads to a museum in Principe Real. The large stone building is divided into two tiers by a grey metal mezzanine and can be quite cold in winter. Whether you're in search of a satisfying dinner or eager to sink a few bottles of wine, Enoteca comes highly recommended.

Food 8, Service 8, Atmosphere 8

Estufa Real, Jardim Botanico da Ajuda, Calçada do Galvao.
Tel: 21 361 9400
Open: 12.30–3.15pm (4pm Sunday). Closed Saturday.   €45

This converted 300-year-old greenhouse enjoys peaceful surroundings in one of Lisbon's oldest botanical gardens. Used primarily as a function venue, over time Estufa Real has built up a solid reputation on the restaurant circuit. It's an ideal daytime choice; sunlight pours through the giant glass windows and spills onto the wicker furnishings within. The creeping trellises and exotic flora of the gardens are the perfect antidote to city life. Any sense of urgency dissipates immediately and reality seems a forgotten concern. Only lunch is served, although dinners can be arranged for groups of 30 or more. But it's the extravagant Sunday buffet that proves to be the main draw for customers.

Well-to-do families spanning the generations venture out to feast on a spread that reaches almost banquet proportions. Expect to find tables occupied for several hours as diners savour an unlimited supply of food. And if Cupid happens to shoot his arrow, wedding receptions can be arranged for around €150 (£100) a head. A culinary event.

Food 8, Service 7, Atmosphere 8

Galeria, Rua de São Bento 334, Estrêla.
Tel: 21 395 2552
Open: 12.30–2.30pm Tuesday–Friday;
8pm–12am Monday–Saturday.   €50

Don't expect to find the traditional fare of pizza and pasta in this Italian restaurant. Milanese chef Augusto Gemelli prides himself on creative cuisine and has developed his own modern menu using classic Italian ingredients. Dishes such as squid ink risotto sit comfortably alongside wild strawberries bathed in balsamic vinegar. As he has worked and travelled all over the world, there is a heavy international influence to Augusto's cooking and spices feature frequently. Fusion cuisine of this calibre is largely unheard of in Portugal, which accounts for the slightly higher price-tag. A popular haunt for couples in search of fine dining, the atmosphere is at times suffocating. Space is cramped and incidental opera music overly dramatic. Nevertheless, the food is exquisite and the décor inoffensively modern. A sensory journey for even

the most travelled of palates.

Food 9, Service 9, Atmosphere 6

Galeto, Avenida da Republica 14, Saldanha.
Tel: 21 356 0269
Open: 7.30am–3am daily   €15

If ever Quentin Tarantino were to shoot a movie in Portugal, this late-night dining den would be top of his location list. The brown varnished bar tops and brass-studded walls are a tribute to 1960s nostalgia. Its opening hours make this the perfect place to refuel midway on a drunken night out, or enjoy a post-club early morning breakfast. The menu is vast, but not for the health-conscious: even the triple-decker club sandwiches undergo a deep-fried treatment. But who can complain when the surroundings are this good? All manner of characters, from neon-clad clubbers to lonely middle-aged men in search of social absolution, perch nonchalantly on the beige leather bar stools. Glass cabinets filled with crockery and men's moccasins complete the

bizarre snapshot. Service is speedy and the air laden with possibility. The spot to contemplate your next novel.

Food 7, Service 8, Atmosphere 9

Gambrinus, Rua das Portas de Santo Antão 23–25.
Tel: 21 342 1466
Open: noon–1.30am daily   €60

There's no better place to sample seafood and hops than Gambrinus – that's if you have the budget to break! Borrowing its name from the God of beer, this beer house with fine dining pretensions is at present the only restaurant in Lisbon with a coveted Michelin star. The range of locally caught seafood is impressive and boasts creatures long-forgotten from the deep. Staff, robed in purple velvet waistcoats (unbelievably, there are 65 of them in total!), take their business extremely seriously and each dish can be tailored to specific wishes. There are two entrances to Gambrinus, one to a sit-down restaurant (complete

with concierge), the other to a less formal saloon-style bar. The latter is more suitable for lunchtime crowds and late-night diners. Exotic wood panelling provides a 'home-from-home' for the politicians and men of letters who occupy the crisp linen-covered tables. This place makes all other mere mortal *cervejarias* look like McDonald's. Recommended, if your idea of heaven is a lightly buttered langoustine on a porcelain plate.

Food 9, Service 9, Atmosphere 9

Kais, Avenida 5 de Outubro 56–1, Alcântara.
Tel: 21 393 2930 www.kais.com.pt
Open: 8pm–2am daily   €35

Owned by the team behind clubs Kremlin and Kapital (as indicated by the giant free-standing letter K outside), this successful dockside restaurant attracts a well-heeled clientele. Similar in both attitude and style to nearby Alcântara Café (see page 62), Kais is very much locked in the 1980s yuppie spirit of status and glamour. A former tram warehouse, the vast space is split into two related but distinct restaurants. Upstairs the emphasis is on

fine international dining, where customers dress to impress. Slick-styled waiters wear a stern expression and the smell of dollar bills hangs heavily in the air. It's certainly something special. Downstairs, the atmosphere is more relaxed and the long wooden tables are frequently filled with large groups. Diners pick and choose from a buffet selection of 40 Portuguese dishes delivered to the table over the course of the evening – and all for only €17 a head. Quality food in up-market company makes this the businessman's choice.

Food 8, Service 9, Atmosphere 8

Lisboa Noite, Rua do Norte 68, Bairro Alto.
Tel: 21 346 8557
Open: 7.30pm–1am. Closed Sunday.   €35

Owned by the same team, this seafood restaurant is a finer dining version of Sinal Vermelho next door. The food is fairly similar and the main difference lies in the décor and clientele. One of the few remaining Pombaline structures in Bairro Alto, the building was once a stable for horses: ring chains and an original well still exist. In 1964 the structure was remodelled as a *fado* house, which functioned up until two years ago when the Sinal team

took over. Now china plates replace nose bags and there are glass goblets instead of troughs. The bright orange walls, decorated with artistic photos of Lisbon by night, are textbook interior design. Although at times a little staid, service is friendly and polite: favoured customers are treated to a glass of vintage cognac after their meal, which the owners allegedly found in a cellar while renovating the building. A calmer and more sophisticated alternative to the bustling eateries of Bairro Alto.

Food 7, Service 8, Atmosphere 7

Mercado de Santa Clara, Campo Santa Clara, Graça.
Tel: 21 887 3986
Open: 12.30–2.30pm, 8–10.30pm. Closed Monday.   €25

Mercado de Santa Clara is part of the market hall that plays centre stage to the Feira da Ladra flea market on Tuesdays and Sundays, but there is nothing second-rate about this loft space restaurant. In stark contrast to the busy early morning cafés, the pace is more metered and subdued. Ceilings are low and the room could be stifling on a hot day, but stunning views of the neighbouring Panteão Nactional de Santa Engrácia are well worth a lunchtime visit. Slightly worn furnishings and aged tile flooring smack of a much-loved premises where little alteration has been made over the years. Food is simple, but abundant in flavour and way beyond the standards of usual home cooking. Gourmet chef Carlos Braz Lopes also runs culinary courses in his 'Cozinhomania' cooks' shop on the other side of the city. The restaurant is a popular choice for Sunday lunch, where a finely attired elderly crowd queue to pile their plates with a traditional Portugese *feijoada* buffet. As close as it gets to Yorkshire pudding and roast potatoes.

Food 8, Service 8, Atmosphere 7

Mezza Luna, Rua da Artilheria Um 16, Rato
Tel: 21 387 9944
Open: 12.30–3pm, 7.30–11pm.
Closed Saturday lunch and Sunday.   €35

Further uptown, but still within walking distance of the Avenida hotels and designer boutiques, this up-market Italian serves traditional pizza and pasta dishes. During the day, it's a popular haunt for smart businessmen and ladies of leisure. By night, well-dressed couples frequent. The Neapolitan chef, who formerly owned a restaurant in New York, set up shop in Lisbon five years ago. He is well respected by both punters and pundits alike and the restaurant has performed consistently well ever since. Dishes are tasty, but nothing overly adventurous, leaving it a safe bet for the tamer of taste buds. Portions are small: the focus is on flavour. Ingredients are top shelf and mozzarella arrives fresh from the motherland every two days. On Fridays, a special of black squid ink linguine with lobster is served and reservations are essential. An ideal pit-stop for hungry shoppers who prefer to fill their wardrobes rather than their stomachs.

Food 7, Service 7, Atmosphere 8

Nariz Apurado, Rua da Esperança 100–102, Madragoa.
Tel: 21 396 0653
Open: 1–3pm, 8pm–2am. Closed Saturday lunch and Sunday. €20

A warm welcome awaits every customer at this friendly modern bistro. Located in the residential streets of Madragoa, slightly off the beaten bar tracks of Santos, the restaurant enjoys little passing trade and relies mainly on regulars. A menu of fresh fish and traditional Portuguese fare is nothing extraordinary, but delicious and well priced. Exhibitions of artwork and photography temporarily fill the muted space and a soundtrack of wistful downbeat music instantly creates a relaxed environment. By night the pace picks up and the restaurant is a popular choice for large dinner groups of young people. The humble Portuguese–Cape Verdean family who

run the place are a refreshing antidote to most restaurant owners: not a note of pretension hangs in the air. A laid-back lunch option.

Food 7, Service 8, Atmosphere 7

Nariz do Vinho Tinto, Rua do Conde 75, Lapa.
Tel: 21 395 3035
Open: noon–3pm, 7pm–midnight. Closed Monday.   €35

This food-lover's haven opened several years ago to rapturous reviews. Owner José Matos Cristovão, one-time editor of *Epicuro* magazine, had friends in plenty of high places and ensured their bottoms were planted firmly on his dining-room seats. Since his death two years ago, the restaurant has passed over to his less

vivacious brother and the atmosphere is consequently more reserved. However, the standard of cooking is still high and you'd be hard-pushed to find a restaurant where the food is more lovingly revered. The menu is varied and traditional dishes are prepared with top-of-the-range ingredients – there's even a choice of different olive oils to accompany meals. The wine list is equally epic and could challenge even the most knowledgeable of wine lovers. In fact the only thing missing from this pleasant restaurant is fun and laughter. Diners tend to be middle-aged types, who probably read about the place in a *Sunday Times* supplement. If *Playboy* were a cook book, this would be it.

Food 8, Service 8/9, Atmosphere 6/7

Oliviers, Rua do Teixeira 35, Bairro Alto.
Tel: 21 342 1024
Open: 8pm–1.30am. Closed Sunday.   €35

Having a TV chef for a father is a good head start in the restaurant business. But Olivier has built a successful business based on merit and his reputation for gastronomic excellence is well founded. The moneyed, beautiful and famous can't seem to get enough of his eclectic combinations. The menu is set and based on a *tapas* style of dining. Each dish is sensational in both taste and texture, and bears testimony to his creative flair in the kitchen. Olivier strives tirelessly to please his guests and waits

expectantly for their verdict on new dishes. Expect to sip pink soup from a martini glass or salivate over goat's cheese dipped in honey. The chef's speciality is a moist chocolate cake wrapped in a thin crust with a delicate cherry sauce. A true professional, he never reveals his recipes. The restaurant is consistently busy and a popular choice for weekend revellers. Definitely where it's at to eat.

Food 9, Service 8, Atmosphere 9

Os Corvos, Beco do Alfurja 4, Alfama.
Tel: 21 888 4508
Open: noon–3pm, 7.30–11.30pm.
Closed Monday and Tuesday.   €28

A stylish modern interior and sophisticated menu make Os Corvos a unique find in Alfama, an area largely characterized by *trascas* and 'tipico' *fado* houses; 'find' being the operative word. Many of the labyrinthine streets of Lisbon's oldest *Bairro* don't even register on maps and it's all too easy to take the wrong turn. But give the restaurant a call, and sympathetic staff are more than happy to collect stranded newcomers. And the superb service doesn't end there: English-speaking waiter Paulo uses a cook's picture book to explain the menu and illustrate delicious and adventurous dishes. Unfortunately, sterile fluorescent strip lights and a conspicuous lack of music detract

from an otherwise warm welcome. But don't let that put you off. A generous wine rack (where supermarket brands sit comfortably alongside classic vintages) and exotic home-made sorbets make it well worth the trek. This is one of the few good restaurants open on a Sunday.

Food 9, Service 9, Atmosphere 6/7

Pap' Açorda, Rua da Atalaia 57, Bairro Alto.
Tel: 21 346 4811
Open: 12.30–2.30pm, 8–11.30pm.
Closed Monday and Sunday.
€45

Chandeliers sparkle and flower petals glisten behind the thick velvet curtains of this Bairro Alto stalwart. It's a world apart from the ramshackle streets outside and only the hallowed few with the foresight to book a table may enter. Ask any Lisboeta to name their favourite restaurant and Pap' Açorda will more than likely come up trumps. From hoteliers to humble students, this is the place everyone is talking about. A former training ground for the team behind Bica do Sapato, the restaurant takes its name from a speciality dish of *açorda* (a stale bread and garlic mixture that bears a disturbing resemblance to baby food) with prawn. A home-made thick viscous chocolate pudding, served directly from the mixing-bowl with a ladle, is also something to write home about. That's if you get the chance! Unfortunately, both the best food and service are reserved for locals and VIPs: uptight

and self-important waiters are unlikely to give you the time of day if they hear an English accent. Shame. Worth checking to see what the fuss is about, but don't settle for second-rate service.

Food 7, Service 5, Atmosphere 8

Pinoquio, Praça dos Restauradores 79–80, Avenida.
Tel: 21 346 5106
Open: 12pm–1am daily   €35

There are plenty of *cervejerias* to choose from in central Lisbon, all of varying quality and price. Pinoquio is the locals' choice. Found directly behind Restauradores metro station, the restaurant is within easy walking distance from the Baixa and main city squares. Unchanged since the 1970s, the neon-lit, mantis-green interior is strangely alluring, albeit headache-inducing. More disturbing still, waiters are dressed in exact colour-match shirts. But don't be put off: the waist-size of returning customers alone is testimony to the satisfying food in store. The seafood selection is limited, but fresh and well prepared. Staff are both polite and informed, and the service is sharp. There are six different beers available and the wine selection is good. The lurid picture-postcard desserts, however, are probably best avoided. A good central option for a no-frills, boozy feast with friends.

Food 8, Service 8, Atmosphere 7

Porco Pretto, Rua Marcos Portugal 5, Rato.
Tel: 21 396 4895 www.porcopreto.com
Open: 12.30–3pm, 8pm–midnight.
Closed Saturday lunch and Sunday. €33

Fans of *Babe* should avoid this place at all costs! Aside from one token fish dish, the menu consists solely of pork. But don't expect bangers and mash! All dishes are made with Iberian pork – a national delicacy – delivered twice a week from the Alentejo. The flavour of this black meat is supposedly enhanced by allowing pigs to roam freely. The meat itself is simple, salted and grilled, but is served with an array of different sauces and vegetables baked in foil bundles. Part of the tranquil Praça das Flores, the restaurant enjoys agreeable surroundings and attracts a number of business clients from the nearby design district. The interior is a mixture of wicker furnishings and brushed metal surfaces, akin to a Habitat showroom. Giant photographs of live pigs hang somewhat disconcertingly alongside cured hams. Quirky touches, such as flowerpots filled with cabbage, add a hint of humour to the room.

Food 7, Service 8, Atmosphere 8

Primavera, Travessa da Espera 34, Bairro Alto.
Tel: 21 342 0477
Open: noon–3pm, 7–11pm. Closed Sunday. €25

Along with nearby 1 da Maio, Primavera is the best example of good, honest Portuguese cooking the city has to offer. The menu is reassuringly simple, but certainly not lacking in skill. Even the most traditional of Lisbon housewives are envious of Senhor Manuel and his kitchen. Like many of the Bairro Alto restaurants,

space is limited: it would be impossible to swing a flea, let alone a cat in this floodlit shoe-box. Still, it makes for a friendly, intimate environment and catching the waiter's attention is never a problem. Delicious smells waft from the spotless kitchen, which is fully on display. If the wait for food proves too torturous, why not try and decipher the proverbs inscribed on the *azulejos* that fill the back walls? The mainly middle-aged crowd is mixed but relaxed. It always seems to be bustling, so it's good for those normally quieter mid-week and early evening meals.

Food 8, Service 8, Atmosphere 7

Ramiro, Avenida Almirante Reis, Estefania.
Tel: 21 885 1024
Open: noon–1am. Closed Tuesday.   €30

Beer on tap is still a relatively new trend in Lisbon, but a half-pint and a plate of seafood are commonplace in the numerous *cervejerias* across town. After 51 years of business, Ramiro is still a favourite with locals from all walks of life. White-collar workers rub shoulders with White House representatives and get their hands dirty with a crab stick or two. The atmosphere is relaxed and the air thick with lively conversation and sticky buttered lobster meat. A more refined upstairs dining area is available for those who prefer to use forks rather than fingers. Despite a less than salubrious location, locals regularly queue for a space on the much-coveted plastic tables. The pick'n'mix menu is varied and the different shellfish are mainly sold by weight. However, staff are happy to advice on quantities. Much of the shellfish arrives daily from Portuguese waters, but the Mozambique prawns are delivered frozen. A great place to gorge yourself on fabulous seafood.

Food 8, Service 8, Atmosphere 8

Santo Antonio, Beco de São Miguel, 7, Alfama.
Tel: 21 888 1328
Open: 8pm–1am. Closed Tuesday. €30

A Sunday opening and leafy outdoor terrace are the main draws for this busy Alfama restaurant. Favoured by media workers and artistic types, the atmosphere is satisfyingly relaxed. Long wooden tables encourage customers to interact, and vibrant conversation across flickering candles continues well into the night. Upstairs, customers can opt for more formal dining. Black and white portraits of movie stars swamp the wall space; some were actual visitors. This self-conscious effort to create a bohemian environment works surprisingly well. The restaurant takes its name from Lisbon's patron saint and a collection of religious statues have been donated over the years. Every June, on the

feast day of Saint Anthony, a big party takes place in the *bairro*. The menu offers a wide selection of *tapas*. Dishes are interesting on paper, but disappointingly don't meet expectations and are a little overpriced. The perfect spot to meet locals and indulge in some intellectual conversation.

Food 6, Service 8, Atmosphere 8

Sinal Vermelho, Rua das Gaveas 89, Bairro Alto.
Tel: 21 346 1252
Open: 12.30–3pm, 7.30–11.30pm. Closed Sunday.   €30

Of the many restaurants in Bairro Alto, the red-fronted Sinal Vermelho is a popular choice for those wanting to line their stomachs before hitting the nearby bars. A young crowd creates an upbeat atmosphere and T-shirt clad staff make for a relaxed environment. Despite the bright jaundice-inducing lighting and an uninspiring interior, there's a definite buzz about the place. Given the modern attitude of the owners, it's surprising to learn that Sinal has been serving customers for 20 years. The restaurant is always busy at weekends and is a popular meeting-place for bright young things. Dishes are simple but delicious and offer some light relief to the usual calorie-laden menus. Fresh seafood and grilled meats won't weigh too much on the belly – particularly important if you've planned big night ahead.

Food 8, Service 8, Atmosphere 8

Solar dos Nunes, Rua 205 Lusiadas 68–72, Alcântara.
Tel: 21 364 7359 www.solardosnunes.restaunet.pt
Open: noon–4pm, 7pm–midnight. Closed Sunday.   €30

Considered to be the bread-basket of Portugal, the Alentejo has taken on an almost mythical quality. Patriotic Portuguese refer to this southern region as a promised land, where pork and fine wines pour forth in place of bread and honey. Solar Dos Nunes prides itself on this heritage and is probably the city's best exam-

ple of straightforward but up-market Alentejian cooking.
Countless magazine articles and glowing reviews hang like tro-
phies on the cluttered walls, alongside cauldron-sized cooking
pots and cured hams suspended from the ceiling. This country-
kitchen environment is instantly inclusive, and the meals pleasantly drawn out. The restaurant is popular with an older generation of sentimental traditionalists, whose eyes are easily the size
of their big bellies. Portions are generous and fish and game are
sold by the kilo. This is where the Portuguese go to be tourists
in their own country.

Food 8, Service 8, Atmosphere 8

Sua Excelência, Rua do Conde 34, Lapa.
Tel: 21 390 3614
Open: 1–3pm, 8–10.30pm.
Closed Saturday and Sunday lunches and Wednesday.   €45

Locals regard this well-established restaurant as part of the city's
furniture. Its reputation is based partly on the high standards of
cuisine and partly on the eccentricities of the owners. Following
the 1974 revolution, Francisco Queiroz returned from Angola
and brought with him a memory-bank of favourite family recipes.
He's not a trained chef, but his expertise lies in flavouring. To
demonstrate his mental dexterity further, Francisco recites the
mouth-watering menu in six different languages. Cooking

methods are described in devastating detail, making any dish difficult to resist. It's an impressive performance for a man of 80. But don't mention politics: strongly right-wing, Francisco has been known to send left-wing sympathizers scuttling from the restaurant. Stranger still, the bar is managed by an ex-commander of the Portuguese marines. The restaurant itself sits somewhere between a domestic jungle and a wedding marquee. Explanation for the multitude of spider plants and creeping vines lies in Francisco's love of botany. The restaurant closes frustratingly early and is best reserved for a quiet night out midweek.

Food 9, Service 9, Atmosphere 7

Sushi Bar, Avenida Infante Dom Henrique, Armazém B.
Tel: 21 881 0320 www.bicadosapato.com
Open: 7.30pm–1am. Closed Sunday.   €28

Part of John Malkovich's Bica do Sapato restaurant, this balcony sushi bar is an ideal choice for those in search of a stylish but swift pre-club pit stop. The menu extends way beyond traditional sushi and *sashimi* dishes, and attempts to recreate a culinary fusion first embarked upon when the Portuguese entered Japanese lands in 1542. On paper the concept sounds great; in reality it's slightly disappointing. A whirlwind of creative flavours collide and compete for attention, resulting in an upsetting absence of taste. As far as sushi goes, it's only marginally better

than Prêt à Manger or Marks & Spencer's Bento Box. That said, those dishes are immaculately prepared works of art and could even outshine the fashion-conscious cliques who dine. Like the restaurant downstairs the atmosphere is lively, but suited to smaller groups. A light start to a heavy night.

Food 7, Service 7, Atmosphere 8

Tasquina da Adelaide, Rua do Patrocínio 70–74, Lapa.
Tel: 21 396 2239
Open: 12.30–3.30pm, 8.30–11.30pm. Closed Sunday.   €35

Based on the concept of the *tasca*, a traditional Portuguese eating house, this intimate restaurant in Campo de Ourique serves up traditional hearty dishes with a touch of sophistication. The culinary skills of charismatic chef Adelaide have attained an almost mythical status. A former shoe-shop owner, Adelaide turned her talents to cooking 10 years ago, inspired by dishes she'd had as a child. Combined with a well-travelled palate and a fetish for experimenting with flavours, this self-made chef creates tasty basic dishes with an extraordinary twist. Her secret ingredient is an olive oil from D'oro, her home town in northern Portugal. International singers, diplomatic figures and straight-up food lovers flock to feast and bestow gifts: a wonderfully bizarre and slightly grotesque birdsong chiming clock was a present from the ambassador of Brazil. Competition to fill the 24 places is

fierce, and don't be surprised to lose a table reservation if you're over 5 minutes late. A hefty but inspired meal.

Food 9, Service 7, Atmosphere 7

Tavares Rico, Rua da Misericórdia, 37, Bairro Alto.
Tel: 21 342 1112
Open: 12.30–14.30pm Tuesday–Friday, Sunday;
7.30–11.30pm Tuesday–Thursday, Sunday;
7.30–10.30pm Friday–Saturday. Closed Monday.   €65

This opulently gilded restaurant once boasted the title of Lisbon's most expensive and luxurious dining house. Founded in 1784, it was favoured by aristocratic types and city notables. However, suffocated by the hands of anachronism, it was forced to close for several years until a change in ownership breathed new life into the golden pillars, and now Tavares is enjoying renewed popularity. The gold and mirrored interior remains true to form, although the clientele are far more varied. Fine diners flock to sample the cooking of former Ritz chef Joaquim

Figugirgdo, young crowds enjoy the novelty of a fine dining experience, while older regulars come to reminisce – although waiters no longer serve them by the mouthful! The atmosphere is surprisingly relaxed for a restaurant of this stature and the dining experience unique to Lisbon. A right royal feast fit for any prince or princess.

**Varanda Restaurant, Four Seasons Hotel Ritz,
Rua Rodrigo da Fonseca 88, Rato.**
Tel: 21 381 1400 www.fourseasons.com/lisbon
Open: 12.30–3pm, 7.30–10.30pm daily.   €50

Sophisticated gastronomy and an emphasis on the quality of
cuisine have successfully elevated the Varanda beyond a hotel
restaurant. Only chefs of solid reputation are given free reign in
the kitchen, making this a firm favourite with Lisbon's culinary
elite. The carefully crafted menu caters for all tastes and
appetites and includes both four- and seven-course *degustation*
menus and an alternative à la carte option. The precision
involved in selecting appropriate wines and complementary food
combinations verges on the obsessive, but it's a treat for any
food fanatic. Given the quality of food and service, it's a shame
that the restaurant persists in keeping a stiff upper lip. A younger
crowd are deterred by the strict black tie policy, while the overtly refined environment can be painfully austere. Best kept for a
romantic dinner or a midweek meal with the parents.

Viagem de Sabores, Rua São João da Praça 103, Sé.
Tel: 21 887 0189
Open: 8–11pm (midnight Friday–Saturday). Closed Sunday.   €28

The neighbouring Romanesque Sé cathedral provides a loose
theme for this charming restaurant. White prayer clothes are
draped over the carved pew-like seating and a large panelled
wall mounting hints at a stained-glass window effect. But any
tones of religious austerity are reassuringly absent. Gentle candle
light seeps through frosted glass, giving the bare stone archways
an orange glow, while a relaxed crowd of diners gather for civilized conversation. As its name aptly suggests, the restaurant
truly is a journey of flavours. The menu is interestingly eclectic

and fuses Thai, French and Portuguese cooking. There's also a
choice of vegetarian options – practically unheard of in carnivo-
rous Portugal! The wine list is selective and of a high standard.
The kitchen staff are commendably efficient at the busiest of
times, and not a note of frenzy hangs in the air. This can be a
cleansing experience for both the palate and the soul!

Food 7, Service 8, Atmosphere 8

XL, Calçada da Estrêla 57–63, Estrêla.
Tel: 21 395 6118
Open: 8pm–midnight Monday–Wednesday;
8pm–2am Thursday–Saturday. Closed Sunday.   €40

Since opening eight years ago, XL has gained a loyal following among Lisbon's moneyed gastronomic elite. In fact, much of the menu remains static as any attempts to modify are met with fierce protests from regulars demanding their favourite dishes. Diners ring a doorbell to enter, but are made to feel like guests the moment they step inside. Colonial-inspired décor and a cosy backroom bar make this feel more like an inclusive country club. A mixed crowd of politicians, celebrities and American Express Gold Card holders let their hair down in the comfort of someone else's dinner party. Tables fill up quickly and reservations are recommended. Charismatic owner Vasco hosts the front of house, while his wife Claudia deftly commands the kitchen. The food is hearty and hellishly tasty desserts are not for the calorie-shy. An extensive wine list boasts some of the best Portuguese bottles in town and fine imported spirits from Russia and beyond. The atmosphere is lively and by 10pm the restaurant is filled with cigar smoke and peels of laughter. Be prepared to leave with a full belly and a stumble in your step.

Food 9, Service 8, Atmosphere 9

drink...

Self-confessed party animals, Lisboetas love to go out but they hate to sit down. Consequently most bars in the city are standing-room only, and a place for a beer and a quiet chat is difficult to find. Locals tend to relax in restaurants before heading to bars in the early hours; some (including Bica do Sapato, Lisboa Noite and Kais) have designated cocktail lounges. Many cafés also have a drinks licence and remain open until late.

The hub of night-time activity is the Bairro Alto, whose narrow backstreets are brimming with bars. Inconspicuous by day, many have no name or discernable features. Because of the hot weather and lack of space, crowds tend to gather on the pavements outside. Up until recently cars zipped in and out of the back alleys, but fortunately the area is now fully pedestrianized. Several shop doorways function as nondescript watering-holes with a take-away policy, often at dirt-cheap prices. The area attracts a myriad of characters, from goths, rastas and skaters to students and media whores. These social groups tend to congregate around different blocks: the top end of Rua de Diário de Notícias is usually populated by less desirable types and under-age drinkers who swill beer by the gallon; conversely the bottom end attracts a discerning media crowd. If in doubt, head for the area between Cafédiário and Fragil.

Originally a military area, Bairro Alto has always supported a bar culture. However, the 1974 revolution saw the dawn of sexual liberation and a flourishing gay scene. A key instigator in this process was Manuel Reis, an entrepreneurial air steward who opened a furniture shop on Rua da Atalaia followed by the hugely successful Fragil. Since then Reis has moved on to pastures new in the Santa Apolónia, taking with him the life and soul of the party. That said, the streets are still consistently busy and an 'anything goes' attitude to cannabis smoking continues to prevail.

Much of Lisbon's older bar architecture owes a toast to eccentric interior designer, Luis Pinto Coelho. During the 1970s he decked out a number of bars in his wonderfully kitsch and unmistakable style (Pavilhão Chinês, Paródia and Procópio). During the Salazar years, the seedy streets of Cais do Sodré were popular with foreigners arriving at the port. A regeneration of the docks in the early 1990s led to a plethora of bar developments. The Santos and Avenida 24 de Julho areas attract a far younger crowd, while the Jardim do Tobacco and Doca de Santo Amaro are a mass of identikit bars, none of notable worth.

Beer-drinking is a relatively new trend in Portugal and only two brands, Sagres and Super Bock, are available on tap, although foreign bars such as O'Gilin's boast a greater international variety. Drinks are served in a less-than-average 20cl tall glass, but a *caneca* (half litre) can be provided on special request. Another drinking delicacy to sample is *ginjinha* – a sweet cherry liqueur. Old men and street urchins gather round barrel bearers in Rossio (A Ginjinha and Ginjinha Popular, both open 7am–midnight) for a shot of the stuff. If nothing else, it's a great cure for the common cold!

121, Rua do Norte 121, Bairro Alto.
Tel: 96 242 7492
Open: 9.30pm–4am. Closed Sunday and Monday.

A new addition to the Bairro Alto bar scene, this popular hang-out attracts jaded locals tired of the same old spots. Large scatter cushions and countless tea lights litter the surprisingly large space. But it's the clientele who provide the most interesting decoration: film producers mingle with seasoned crusties and men in suits during the course of an evening. It's the true epitome of Lisbon's eclectic social scene. Accordingly, the possibilities for an evening out are endless. Expect to find yourself embroiled in conversation about art-house movies one minute and political corruption the next. The atmosphere is deceptively electric given the mediocre surroundings and the bar's lack of distinctive character. Changing exhibitions also rotate bi-monthly. Spacious enough for a quiet drink, but best enjoyed when packed to the rafters.

Agito, Rua da Rosa 261, Bairro Alto.
Tel: 21 343 0622
Open: 6pm–2am. Closed Monday.

Literally translated, '*agito*' is a Brazilian word inciting action and movement. Sandwiched between a cluster of jazz bars at the top end of Rua da Rosa, this striking bar is as far from the madding

crowd as a Bairro Alto drinking spot can be. But the mood is nonetheless vibrant. Walls are daubed with lively blocks of colour and bamboo curtains hang from the doorway. A mural depicting a cartoon cow showering unsuspecting city folk with milk from its udders is difficult to miss and has become a defining icon for the bar. Further seating can be found in the glass conservatory out back. Food is served, with many veggie-friendly options available but is nothing extraordinary. Chilled and effortlessly cool.

Baliza, Rua da Bica de Duarte Belo, Bairro Alto.
Tel: 21 347 8719
Open: 1pm–2am Monday–Friday; 4pm–2am Saturday.
Closed Sunday.

Together with Bicaense and hairdressers WIP, this small café-bar

has forged an increasingly cool community at the top of the Elevador da Bica. It was once a traditional football *tasca*; 'baliza' is Portuguese for 'goal'. By day, students and contemplative types bury themselves in thought or a good novel. The sounds of a percolator hissing and the funicular trundling up and down the hill are as reassuring as clockwork. After dark, the serene atmosphere picks up as unpretentious creatives flit between here and Bicaense. Changing works of art keep the décor fresh and the mood is consistently inspirational. Friendly staff and tasty *tostas* put Baliza in a league of its own.

Berim Bar, Rua das Praças 11, Baixa.
Tel: 21 397 3451
Open: 11pm–late daily

A stone's throw from the bars and clubs of Santos, this homely drinking-hole has been serving night owls for 20 years. The bar only closes once the last customer has left, and this can be any time between 6 and 10am. An equally relaxed kitchen stays open, serving a selection of traditional Portuguese food. But late-night munchies come at a price: a steak will set you back nearly €30! Still, it's a classier alternative to the greasy kebab stands that line the streets nearby. Decanters filled with whisky and sinister china dolls in glass cabinets create a setting that lies somewhere between a private gentlemen's club and Mavis from Basildon's front room. Slurred hypotheses on the meaning of life are interrupted only by the tinkling of piano keys and gentle strumming

from a guitar: live *fado* music takes place three nights a week.

Bicaense, Rua da Bica Duarte Belo 38–42, Bairro Alto.
Tel: 21 325 7940
Open: 7pm–2am. Closed Sunday and Monday.

Positioned at the top end of the Elevador da Bica, this laid-back
lounge bar is a favourite with cool and collected Lisboetas.
Friendly owner and man-about-town Mikas was responsible for
the immensely popular (but now defunct) bar-cum-hairdressers,
WIP. His personal collection of clocks and film projectors dominate the front room, whose marble walls are over 100 years old.
This area, which Mikas refers to as his 'past', was once a *tasca* (a
traditional Portuguese drinking-hole). 'The Future', a large room

(for Lisbon) that lies next door, is a carefully configured comfort
zone. Giant beanbags fill the floor space and rainbow-coloured
lights can be dimmed to reflect the atmosphere. Regular art exhibitions adorn the walls, and film projections roll over a soundtrack provided by a different DJ every night. A mixed crowd of
arty types, clubbers and local shop owners gather to enjoy the
latest in hip house and future soul. Fun and unpretentious.

Café de São Bento, Rua de São Bento 212, São Bento.
Tel: 21 395 2911
Open: 6pm–2am daily

If you're in search of a midnight snack more substantial than a hot-dog and tastier than yesterday's bread, head for this classy backroom bar on the Rua de São Bento. Far more up-market than nearby Snob, it has the same gentleman's club feel. From the outside, frosted windows and the crisp clinking of crystal wine glasses can be intimidating. But the doorbell entry system is simply for show: practically anyone can get in. Popular with politicians from the parliament buildings over the road, the bar is famous for its late-night *bife a marrare* steaks, served until 1am. As the café has been in business for 22 years, it's a dish they've had time to perfect. Of late, the bar has fallen into favour with the city's rich kids, who bring light relief to the stuffy surroundings.

Cafédiário, Rua do Diário de Noticias 3, Bairro Alto.
Tel: 21 342 2434
Open: 8pm–3am daily. Closed Sunday.

Of all the bars in Bairro Alto, this one is consistently popular – even on a week night. That's partly because colourful owner Gabriel is friends with half of Lisbon, and partly because it's a damn fine place to drink away an evening. Music comes courtesy of a makeshift stereo system, but an impressive selection of CDs is enough to keep the ambience merry. The brightly coloured bar is small, but most of the action takes place on the pavement between Diário and bar Suave opposite. An 'in' crowd of pleasure-seeking trendsetters from their mid-20s upwards meet here before heading to club Lux.

Caxim Bar, Costa do Castelo 20–22, Graça.
Open: 8pm–2am (4am Friday–Saturday)

Strictly one for those in the know, this inconspicuous bar goes almost undetected by day; most non-regulars only stumble upon it by chance. Morrocan in flavour, the dimly lit interior is an Aladin's cave of coloured lanterns and smoking paraphernalia; stepping over the threshold is like crossing into a whole new continent. The unmistakable smell of hash wafts around the room, thanks to the liberal attitude of Caxim's owners. But don't expect to make a purchase on the premises – it's BYO only. Inevitably, Caxim is a popular student haunt although a cross-section of characters drifts in throughout the night. The atmos-

phere is certainly conspiratorial but in no way exclusive: conversations between strangers are common, so don't go expecting a quiet drink! Herbal teas and mystical beverages are served alongside the standard bottles of beer and a limited menu will keep those post-smoking munchies at bay. A wonderful den of iniquity.

Clube da Esquina, Rua da Barroca 30–32, Bairro Alto.
Tel: 21 342 7149
Open: 4.30pm–2am Monday–Saturday; 9.30pm–2am Sunday

A bar with seating is a rare find in Bairro Alto; a bar open during the day is almost unheard of. But Clube da Esquina is that welcome anomaly. More civilized than most drinking-holes in the area, it attracts a crowd too old to loiter on street corners and too young to stay at home. Mint-green shutters open out onto the street and window seats are quickly snapped up by early-evening drinkers; dog-eared film posters and flyers detailing up-coming gigs flutter in the breeze. As the night draws on, the outside area is a throng of activity. Resident DJs spin jazz and soul to the musically discerning crowd. Instantly welcoming, and catering for all types and tastes.

Costa do Castelo Bar das Imagens, Calçada Marquês de Tancos 1, Graça.
Tel: 21 888 4636
Open: 4pm–2am Thursday–Saturday; 3–9pm Sunday.
Closed Monday–Tuesday, and throughout January and February.

The veranda outside this lively local hang-out is a wonderful place to watch the sun setting over Lisbon's undulating skyline. Chairs and tables litter the paved area and an outdoor sound system has been rigged up to keep drinkers entertained; a regular DJ spins funk, dub, soul and reggae. The mood is chilled and a complete antithesis to a club environment. Tourists making their way up to the Castelo de São Jorge often stop by for a drink, which inevitably turns into two. Prices are good and the company is always a pleasure. Colourful characters from the neighbouring Chapitô circus school add their own inimitable sense of charm. When temperatures drop, drinkers decamp to tables indoors. The quirky interior is both fun and curious.

Divina Comédia, Largo de São Martnho 6–7, Sé.
Tel: 21 887 5599
Open: 6pm–2am. Closed Monday.

Nestling below the sleepy eves of the Sé cathedral, this pleasant bar offers comfort and calm on a blustery night. It was originally a Brazilian music bar, but a ban on live entertainment necessitated the bar/restaurant transformation. However, the space retains much of its vibrant past in the form of curious furnishings, most notably the plush red sofa and pink feather boa wrapped around a hat-stand, and a Mondrian-inspired colour scheme. These days the mood is more serene. The pace picks up around 11pm, but never accelerates beyond a quiet couple of drinks. It's popular

with a middle-class crowd of artists and free-thinkers, and a wide-screen TV also shows football.

Esplanada do Rio, Rua da Cintura, Cais do Sodré.
Open: 10am–2am daily, May–October. Closed November–April.

A livelier but more down-market equivalent of neighbouring Perudiguous do Rio, this esplanade bar is actually part of the Steakhouse restaurant. But don't let that put you off. Considered a separate entity during summer months, it's a great place to spend a balmy night – especially if Peridiguous is already too busy. Pumping dance music blares from an outdoor sound system and acts as a siren for any young revellers in the area. Am or pm, an upbeat but casual crowd lounges about on bed-size beanbags. Perch on a stool at the 'Club Tropicana' beach bar, and

friendly Lisboetas will instantly engage you in conversation. Officially the bar closes at 2am, although crowds rarely disperse until 4am. Food is served, but is nothing special. Not the spot for a quiet tipple, but a great way to get the party started. Bands perform live every Thursday.

Estado Liquido, Largo de Santos 5a, Santos.
Tel: 21 395 5820 www.estadoliquido.com
Open: 10pm–2am Tuesday–Saturday

Catering for a laid-back but commercial crowd, this open-plan space is more of a dance-floor than a lounge bar. Aside from a few far-flung beanbags, it's standing-room only. At weekends queues stretch along the road (peak time is about 1.30am), although on week nights the bar appears conspicuously empty. Slightly more stylish than the usual mainstream hotspots, Estado Liquido still has aspirations of trend beyond its station. Glitter lava lamps and psychedelic projections are unnecessarily kitsch, while a distracting video screen is a token gesture to an MTV generation. DJs play chill-out and deep house nightly, with live accompaniment on Friday and Saturday nights. Try the house spe-

ciality *morangoska*, a cocktail made with fresh strawberries and vodka. There's no specific dress code, but a potential €50 door charge is a big enough hint to send unwanted guests packing. The Estado team also plans to release a series of branded CDs.

Fluid, Avenida Dom Carlos I 67, Madragoa.
Tel: 21 395 5957 www.fluid-pt.com
Open: 10pm–4am. Closed Sunday and Monday.

Opening three years ago, this fashionable venue has the facilities of a bar and the attitude of a club. At weekends, hip media types cram themselves onto the tiny dance-floor and are more than happy to throw caution to the wind, drenching their Diesel Ts with sweat. Funk classics, soulful house and cutting-edge sounds are the main draw for a bar where music is more than just sonic wallpaper. The 1960s-style interior is predictably textbook-trendy, but deliciously seedy red lighting lends a conspiratorial intimacy. The atmosphere is relaxed, although a little feigned at times, and attitudes can be as brittle as the designer plastic white seating. The bar is often full by 1am and queues can be long, especially if an international DJ is in town.

Fragil, Rua da Atalaia 128, Madragoa.
Tel: 21 346 9578 www.fragil.com
Open: 11.30am–4am. Closed Sunday, and Monday–Tuesday in winter.

When Fragil opened 21 years ago, Bairro Alto was nothing more than a muddle of empty backstreets. The former bread factory quickly became synonymous with a flourishing gay scene and a landmark in Lisbon's night life. In past years popularity has dwindled – mainly because of the departure of Manuel Reis – and this one-time driving engine would probably now have trouble passing its MOT. The décor, largely unchanged, is a cruel reminder of the club's halcyon days and nostalgia hangs heavily in the dark, intimate corners. That said, Fragil is making moves in new directions. Unsigned Portuguese bands play every Wednesday night to a keen crowd of live music fans, while weekends still attract an overwhelmingly gay crowd. The door policy is less exclusive these days and bouncers guarding the cast-iron doors are almost a token gesture to tradition. An interesting indicator of where 'it' once was.

Herois, Calçada do Sacramento 14, Baixa.
Tel: 21 342 0077
Open: noon–2am. Closed Sunday.

Just off the Rua Garratt, this bar/café is a convenient meeting-place for afternoon shoppers and post-work drinkers. Perspex lamps, beige leather benches and plastic seating conforms to a 1960s-inspired theme. The café selection is limited, but it's a pleasant enough space for biding your time. Beanbags on the lower level provide comfortable lounge space beneath the DJ decks, while ample indoor seating is available over two floors; unlike most bars in the city, it's actually possible to sit down and have a drink. At night Herois attracts a gay crowd with an over-stated emphasis on the body beautiful. Drink prices are steep for

the area and the bar is arguably too trendy for its boots.

Lounge Café, Rua da Moeda 1, Cais do Sodré.
Open: 4pm–2am. Closed Monday.

Buried at the bottom of the Elevador da Bica, near the seedy bars of Cais do Sodré, this unpretentious bar is favoured by students, nihilist artists and financially impaired intellectuals. A battered velvet sofa and tatty lampshade self-consciously displayed in the rafters suggest a dishevelled comfort. The dimly lit room is the ideal place to nurse a melancholic pint while lamenting life's woes. Discerning DJs spin a selection of disco, breakbeat and electro, although the crowd is mostly too cool or too jaded to dance. At weekends, though, it's an interesting place to people-watch and feel part of the alternative in crowd, however dwin-

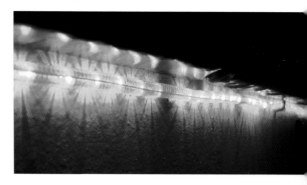

dling it might be. The spray-painted magic mushroom outside has become a local landmark.

Lua, Avenida 24 de Julho, 90b/c, Santos.
Tel: 21 396 1729 www.lualua.net
Open: 8pm–3am. Closed Sunday.

Slightly out on a limb, this welcoming bar and restaurant is one of the few venues still worth a visit on the Santos stretch. Fortunately the under-age drinkers and irritating *bentos* (yuppie rich-kids) have overlooked this spot, instead sticking to their usual neon-lit sports bars. Spread over two floors, it's spacious enough to accommodate large groups of diners quite comfortably. Red walls and aquamarine drapes, illuminated only by can-

dles, create an intimate cave-like atmosphere. The music policy is chill-out, lounge, funk and disco with live music on Friday and Saturday nights. The crowd is laid-back and unpretentious. Not the most inspiring bar in Lisbon, but a nice enough place to kick back for an hour or so.

Madres de Goa, Rua dos Industriais 9, Madragoa.
Tel: 21 396 1413 www.madresdegoa.com
Open: 8am–2.30am Monday–Thursday;
8am–4am Friday–Saturday. Closed Sunday.

Serving customers around the clock, there's never a dull moment in this vibrant café/restaurant/bar. The lively young owners share a disposition almost as sunny as the ethnically inspired interior, making it a pleasurable place to spend time. Daytimes, the café caters for students who stumble in, bleary-eyed, to grab a coffee and croissant before heading to the university over the road. Food is served until 2am, with regular themed nights arranged for large dinner groups. At weekends, DJs perform with live percussion in the intimate bar downstairs. But don't worry if you've left your dancing shoes at home – there are plenty of quiet spots to indulge in conversation and nurse an expertly mixed cocktail. A truly inclusive environment that's difficult to leave.

Majong, Rua da Atalaia 3, Bairro Alto.
Tel: 21 342 1039
Open: 7pm–4am daily

Stepping into this lo-fi, minimalist bar can be like walking into a private house party. Although a key player on the Bairro Alto bar scene, Majong sees itself as a cooler cut above the rest. A somewhat self-important clique of unemployed actors and aspiring artists hang out and discuss 'projects in the pipeline'. Their misplaced optimism is quite infectious (especially after a couple of *caipirinhias*) and the urge to buy into their bohemian lifestyle is difficult to resist. After all, you could be rubbing shoulders with a future Portuguese soap star! Table football is a welcome touch of down-to-earth relief. By 11pm the bar is packed out and chaotic, with plenty of pushing and shoving at the bar.

Mexe, Rua de Trombeta 2a/4, Bairro Alto.
Tel: 21 347 4910
Open: 6pm-3.30am October-March; 9.30-3.30am April-September

This upbeat bar has the large-scale pretensions of a club on a small-scale premises. But size isn't everything, and beat-hungry party animals can still find space to bust a move or two. Music is a mixture of house, hip-hop and more soulful flavours. Metal pillars and pink perspex lanterns provide a backdrop for riotous revelry. A cross-section of multi-ethnic characters frequent; and

it's not unusual to see straight-laced students rubbing shoulders with cred-crazed rudeboys. But there's a reassuring absence of attitude and thankfully punters choose to leave their egos at the door. Loose and relaxed, anything goes in this laid-back bar.

Net Jazz Café, Costa do Castelo 1–7, Graça.
Tel: 21 888 0406
Open: 11am–3am. Closed Monday.

Part of the Chapitô circus school, this cosy bar is accessed via a winding staircase from the upstairs terrace. During the day it functions as an internet café and study area, but on a Friday and Saturday night it's a great place to catch live bands. The music policy is loose, but reliably eclectic, with acts ranging from 1950s swing to African percussion. The focal point is a large marble bath filled with cushions, from which the artists perform. A consistently receptive audience of artists and bohemian students are never afraid to participate, making for a lively atmosphere. The space itself is equally vibrant, with lurid mosaics and barber's chairs forming part of the furniture. An evening at Net Jazz is a truly unique experience. This is the kind of bar you'd love to stumble across anywhere in the world.

O'Gilins, Rua des Remolares 8, Cais do Sodré.
Tel: 21 342 1899
Open: 11am–2am daily

Pints are largely unheard of in Lisbon. Those seeking something more substantial than the standard 20cl thimbleful should head to one of the city's Irish bars. O'Gilins is the oldest and easily the best of the lot. Friendly owner Connor has built up an international client-base of pint-hungry punters. Imported beers on tap are a welcome alternative to the ubiquitous Superbock and Tagus brands and live sport is regularly shown. Traditional Irish bands perform Thursdays, Fridays and Saturdays, and there's a pub quiz on Sundays. Customers are also treated to a fry-up and a cup of real tea (with milk) on Sunday mornings. It's like a home from home. In fact, the only difference is the opening hours.

Paródia, Rua do Patrocínio 2b, Campo de Ourique.
Tel: 21 396 4724
Open: 6pm–2am Monday–Friday; 10pm–2am Saturday

This intimate drinking den lies slightly off the beaten track in the affluent and residential district of Campo de Ourique. Designed by Luis Pinto Coelho, a collector of junk, antiques and art pieces, it opened in the mid-1970s. The name 'Paródia' was taken from a satirical weekly published in the 1900s by artist and writer Rafael Bordalo Pinheiro. The dark and mysterious alcoves became a meeting-place for intellectuals who would gesticulate wildly about matters of abstract philosophy. These days the conversation is far more subdued. Treasured relics, the velvet cushions still hold as many memories as they do dust. Walls are covered

in art nouveau posters and ornate-framed mirrors. Ring a doorbell to enter.

Pavilhão Chinês, Rua Dom Pedro V89, Bairro Alto.
Tel: 21 342 4729
Open: 6pm–2am Monday–Saturday; 9pm–2am Sunday

Love it or loathe it, this undeniably unique bar is cause for conversation. The kitsch and cluttered décor is the unmistakable
handiwork of Luis Pinto Coelho, also responsible for Paródia and
Procópio (see pages 117 and 121). A myriad of rooms are
decked floor-to-ceiling with glass cabinets stuffed full of curios
and odd knick-knacks; collections of toy soldiers stand to attention while porcelain dolls leer menacingly. *En masse*, the effect is
quite grotesque and can turn the stomach after a couple of

creamy cocktails. But the sheer volume of visual stimulation will
remedy any lull in conversation. Lacking any contemporary character, this dusty museum-piece feels stuck in a time-warp and
the stagnant smell of mothballs hangs in the air. But it's still
surprisingly popular with a young crowd. One of the few
spacious bars in Lisbon, with the added bonus of a back-room
pool table.

**Perudiguous do Rio, Rua da Cintura, Armazém 65,
Cais do Sodré.**
Open: 11am–4am daily. Closed November–April.

This sophisticated summer-only 'beach bar' occupies an enviable
spot on the waterfront, 5 minutes' walk from the Cais do Sodré
ferry terminal. By day, there's no better spot to sip a cocktail and
catch a few rays while watching sail boats float along the Tejo.
Those seeking shade can find comfort at one of the many tables
laid out under an awning, while sun-worshippers can opt for a
seaside deck chair. The sound of water lapping over the sun-
baked rocks below is heavenly. Less Southend and more
Seychelles, the bar attracts a wealthy and discerning crowd. As

dusk settles, courting couples meet for a quiet pre-dinner drink
and marvel at the illuminated Cristo Rei statue over the river.
The pace picks up after dark, when the party-hungry local elite
arrive in their droves. Essential for summer socializing.

Portas Largas, Rua da Atalaia 105, Bairro Alto.
Tel: 21 346 6379
Open: 7pm–4am May–October; 8pm–3.30am November–April

This popular Bairro Alto watering-hole was once a rough and ready *tasca*. Despite renovation, the original marble counter and tables remain. An old-fashioned cash register dominates the bar in all its glory, while blue and white tiles add rustic charm. Enjoying a favourable position opposite Fragil, Portas Largas is known traditionally as a gay bar. In recent years the in-crowd has found new breeding-ground, and the bar attracts a mixture of local workers, tourists and casual drinkers. Most choose to slouch with a beer in the doorway; it's a good vantage-point for surveying passers-by. Although endearing, the scruffy interior can feel uncomfortable on a quiet night.

Procópio, Alto de Sao Francisco 21a, Amoreiras.
Tel: 21 385 2851
Open: 6pm–3am Monday–Friday; 9pm–3am Saturday.
Closed Sunday.

The bric-à-brac opulence that characterizes this conspiratorial drinking club is the unmistakable hand of Luis Pinto Coelho. A predecessor to Paródia, it is now owned by his ex-wife Alice. Guests who ring the doorbell are greeted by a friendly cocktail waiter in an ill-fitting dinner suit. It's a surreal experience and a scene even David Lynch could not have imagined. The open-plan bar is larger and brighter than Paródia, but enjoys similar decoration: fringed lampshades cast shards of light onto the exotic wood and plush velvet furnishings. This was once a bubble of frenetic political activity. The energy has since seeped away and the bar itself is as much a collector's piece as the curios housed within. Located in a quiet courtyard near the Jardim das Amoreiras, Procópio is easy to miss. Find it just off the Rua João Penha.

Santiago Alquimista, Rua de Santiago 19, Alfama.
Tel: 21 882 0533/0259
Open: 10am–2am Sunday–Thursday; 10am–4am Friday–Saturday

This deceptively large building below the Castelo de São Jorge was a gift to local art schools Idfic and Arco from the Calouste Gulbenkian foundation. A former blacksmith's, the space took 2 years to reconstruct and features original walls from the castle foundation. The area has been divided into two parts, one a rehearsal space for arts students and the other a theatre/late-night bar. A broad spectrum of events take place nightly, ranging from karaoke contests, stand-up comedy stints, DJ sets and sombre gothic folk gatherings. A venue of this size (600 capacity) with a late weekend licence is a unique find in this sleepy part of town. The crowd, a mix of middle class intellectuals and creatives, is similar to that of nearby Chapitô. An alternative and more cultured take on Lisbon's nightlife.

Side, Rua da Barroca 33, Bairro Alto.
Open: 10am–2am. Closed Sunday.

One of the only Bairro Alto bars where signs of life are evident during both day and night. A slick styled interior and health-conscious selection of lunchtime snacks attract a trendy crowd of local fashion designers and hairdressers. Home-made salads and quiches are delivered daily, with a weekly changing world dish. Delicious fresh fruit juices are available by day, with a more alcoholic menu by night. Like all bars in the area the space itself is small. But the much-coveted window seats make for perfect people-watching. A crowd of vibrant but laid-back media and music types tends to fill the paving area between Side and Clube da Esquina opposite. Side is one of the few bars that offers a good selection by the glass as opposed to the bog-standard

house red and white wines that are normally available.

Snob, Rua do Século 178, Bairro Alto.
Tel: 21 346 3723
Open: 4.30pm–3.30am daily.

In the 30 years since its inception, Snob has always been associated with a journalistic crowd who never leave the office until after dark. A younger generation of scribes has since moved elsewhere, although old-timers still like to sink a beer or two. The green leather booths are conducive to long conversations, often conducted to a soundtrack of raucous laughter. In spite of the drab and fading décor, the atmosphere is still reliably lively. Along with Café de São Bento, Snob is one of the few establishments to offer a late-night menu; expect steak in Madeira sauce or jumbo sausages.

snack...

Like most Europeans, Lisboetas love to drink coffee and eat cakes. There are more *pastelarias* (pastry shops) per 100 yards than there are lamp-posts in Lisbon and it's surprising how practically identical places manage to stay in business. Most serve a range of pastries and cakes (*bolas*) along with more savoury snacks (*salgados*) – the most prevalent being *pasteis de bacalhau* (cod fishcakes) and *rissois de carne* (deep-fried meat patties). The cake selection is almost overwhelming, but there are a few local specialities to look out for: head to Confeitaria Nacional to taste the *bola rei* (traditional Christmas cake), Antiga Confeitaria de Belém for the *pasteis de nata* (custard tarts) and Pasteis de Cerveja for the rather bizarre *pastel de cerveja* (beer cakes).

Ordering a coffee can be equally complicated and trying to decipher the different methods of preparation is a mission in itself. Most Portuguese opt for a *bica* (a short black coffee) which they sweeten with sugar or a *pau de canela* (cinnamon stick). Even stronger is an *italiana* – the equivalent of an espresso. Those after a common *latte* should ask for *um galao*. The main brands of coffee are Nicola and Brasíliera.

Lisbon's first wave of coffee culture came in the early 19th century with the

growth of a literary bourgeoisie, mainly around the Chiado and Baixa districts. Fine examples of traditional tea houses include Café a Brasíleira, Café Nicola and Martinho da Arcada, although Versailles in Saldanha is arguably the most authentic. Sticklers for tradition, the city's old folk continue to gather at 5pm for a game of cards and a devilishly sweet afternoon pastry.

Until recently the café scene has been static, although venues with a more dis-tinguishable character are starting to appear; Café no Chiado and Pãu de Canela offer not only refreshments, but also a place to kick back and watch the world float by. Lisboetas have also acquired a taste for herbal tea, reflected in specialist tea shops such as Cultura do Cha. The distinction between café, bar and shop is often blurred, with many cafés undergoing an after-dark transforma-tion. Several of these, such as Baliza and Madres de Goa, are listed in Drink (see pages 98–123). Esplanadas are often just a kiosk serving limited food and drinks, but several have been included by virtue of their beautiful location.

Antiga Confeitaria de Belém, Rua de Belém 84–92.
Tel: 21 363 7423
Open: 8am–midnight daily

If you're paying a visit to the cultural district of Belém, don't leave without sampling the wares of this world-famous cake shop. Any Lisboeta worth their weight in flaky pasty will agree that this is the best place to savour the national dessert of *pasteis de nata* (custard tarts). Only three bakers know the exact quantities of this top secret recipe, which dates back to the monks of Mosteiro dos Jerónimos of the early 1800s. Each morning at 7am, the bakers lock themselves into the Oficina do Segredo (secret workshop) to prepare the cream and dough. On an average weekday up to 10,000 *pasteis de Belém* are sold and the counter is constantly rammed. There's a take-away service available – you're provided with special paper tubes that will accommodate half a dozen – or, if you prefer, you can take a seat in the blue-tiled interior; but a sprinkling of sugar and cinnamon is essential wherever you eat them.

Arte Café, Rua das Escolas Gerais 17–23, Alfama.
Tel: 21 882 2607/8 www.a-perve.rcts.pt
Open: 2–9pm daily; gallery open 2–8pm daily

This clean-cut café, found in the Alfama backstreets, forms part of a triumvirate of spaces that embraces an art gallery and a

media-lab. The brainchild of Portuguese artists Carlos Cabral Nunes and Nuno Espinho da Silva, the collective was set up with the intention of promoting home-grown contemporary art, including works from the country's ex-colonies in Africa. The space is filled with all manner of sculptures and paintings, which serve as an interesting talking-point. The elegant marble walls once belonged to a butcher's and have been restored and adapted by the owners themselves. An open space out back is available for poetry readings and several computers can be used for study. An obscure location means the café receives little passing trade, but if you're in the area it's definitely worth a visit.

As Vicentinhas, Rua do São Bento 700, Rato.
Tel: 21 388 7040
Open: 4–7pm. Closed Sunday.

Confirming the cliché that little old ladies make good tea and cake, As Vicentinhas serves a home-made spread Mrs Beeton would have been proud to call her own. At the helm of this tea room/religious knick-knack shop is a group of genteel churchgoers who have dedicated their lives equally to the cloth... and the dishcloth. Customers are quite literally invited to take a pew, and nibble on one of the deliciously sticky and stodgy home-made cakes (we recommend the buttery scones). A wide range of teas is stocked, but be prepared to drink whatever the elderly waitress (complete with ill-fitting wig) can remember to bring. And

don't expect to leave in a hurry: a brew can take up to 40 minutes to deliver! Still, it's ample time to study the intriguingly odd shop merchandise; effigies of Jesus and crocheted baby boots can be found alongside framed photos of Hugh Grant and Anthony Quinn torn directly from the pages of *Hello!* magazine. On this occasion it has to be seen to be believed.

Buenas Aires, Calçada (Escadinhas) do Duque n. 31 B.
Tel: 93 661 3672
Open: 6pm–midnight Tuesday–Saturday; 3pm–midnight Sunday.
Closed Monday.

Conveniently situated on the steep hike from Rossio to the bars of Bairro Alto, this bohemian restaurant has been permanently busy since opening in 2002. The bric-à-brac collection of clay

ornaments and iconic film posters belong to the Argentinian owner who has collected them over the years. The musical selection reflects his native origins, along with an interest in traditional *fado*. The space was once a photographic shop and pictures that were once for sale here still hang on the walls. The rough wooden surfaces and warm glowing lanterns have the overtones of a gypsy tavern and are more than welcoming on a rainy day. Artistic types regularly return to enjoy a simple but tasty menu in a low-key setting. One of the few indoor comfort spots open on a Sunday afternoon.

Café Bernard, Rua Garrett 104, Chiado.
Tel: 21 347 3133
Open: 8am–midnight. Closed Sunday.

Bernard has all the trappings of a classic Lisbon tearoom: cream cakes, an industrial-sized coffee machine and hordes of tourists. In terms of decoration and clientele, it's traditional in every sense. At 5pm on the dot, the city's old folk gather for a *crème patisserie* and a game of cards. More expensive outside tables are the reserve of tourists and thirsty shoppers. The café is especially famous for its freshly baked croissants, which are constantly cooked in a fire oven and served with lashings of jam and cream. Service can be slow and austere waiting staff are unnecessarily aloof and self-important.

Café a Brasílieira, Rua Garrett 120, Chiado.
Tel: 21 346 9541
Open: 8am–2am daily

Customers were given a free bag of coffee beans when Brasílieira opened in 1905, as the café is home to the Portuguese coffee brand of the same name. At its 1920s peak, it was an intellectual powerhouse where poets and revolutionaries would put the world to rights over a *bica* and a cream puff. These days it's a tick-box tourist spot for visitors to the city. A bronze statue of Portugal's finest literary export, Fernando Pessoa, proves the main focal point; trigger-happy holiday-makers insist on photographing loved ones draped over the poet. The carved wooden interior is nothing short of magnificent and a well-stocked cake cabinet seems to stretch for miles. At night the esplanade is a hotspot for post-dinner drinks.

Café Nicola, Praça Dom Pedro IV (Rossio) 24–25, Baixa.
Tel: 21 346 0579
Open: 8am–10pm Monday–Friday; 9am–5pm Saturday.
Closed Sunday.

The most central of Lisbon's traditional tea houses, Café Nicola spills out onto the busy Rossio square. Although it is distinguishable by its indulgent Art Deco façade, the recently renovated interior is rather less impressive. Despite the suffocating exhaust fumes and relentless honking of car horns, outdoor tables are permanently occupied. The cake selection is disappointingly limited, with the cream of the crop often devoured by mid-afternoon. Still, customers can sip on their coffees safe in the knowledge that they are surrounded by history. The current premises, opened in 1929, was built on the site of an early 18th-century café favoured by poet Manuel Maria Barbosa du Bocage. It's second to Brasílieira in the coffee-brand stakes, and there are 25 varieties of coffee bean for sale in the branch round the back.

Café no Chiado, Largo do Picadeiro 11–12, Baixa.
Tel: 21 346 0501
Open: 11am–2am. Closed Sunday.

Set above the bustling streets of Chiado, this is an oasis of calm

in Lisbon's trendiest shopping district. Civilized but informal surroundings attract a light-lunch crowd of local workers and media types, who meet to discuss business over a glass of white wine and muted jazz. A menu of salads, steaks, quiche and sandwiches is as refreshingly unpretentious as the clientele and it certainly won't burn a hole in your pocket. Outdoor seating on the cobbled leafy esplanade offers a welcome escape from the blazing midday sun and one of the quietest spots in central Lisbon. After the lunch crowd have disappeared, students and young intellectuals while away the afternoon with a coffee and a good book. There's an impressive range of Portuguese and foreign newspapers on offer and internet access is available at the Ciber Chiado upstairs.

Café No Combro, Calçada do Combro 83, Bairro Alto.
Tel: 21 347 5244
Open: 12–6pm, 8pm–2am. Closed Sunday–Wednesday dinner.

Situated at the quieter end of Calçada do Combro, this fledgling venture lies somewhere between a café and restaurant, mixed with the cool and relaxed atmosphere of a bar. It's set apart from the achingly trendy hang-outs of the Bairro Alto area, but still attracts hip 20-somethings in search of a relaxed bite to eat. The lunch menu is refreshingly light and modern, offering a selection of salads, quiches and fresh juices. By night, you can choose from an interesting selection of Thai and Australasian cuisine. Multi-lingual staff are helpful and friendly, and more than happy

to sit down and chat about Lisbon's nightlife. New generation
cafés of this type are rare in Lisbon and provide a welcome relief
to some of the more stuffy and formal coffee houses.

Café Rosso, Rua Ivens 53–61, Baixa.
Tel: 21 347 1524
Open: noon–1am daily

There are two entrances to this courtyard café in the heart of
Chiado; both are easy to miss. A small passageway opens out
into an open expanse dotted with outdoor tables. Tall stone-
washed buildings on all four sides serve as an effective sound
barrier to the noisy streets outside, but young staff and a predominantly teenage crowd manage to keep the atmosphere
upbeat well into the night. The food menu is fairly standard canteen fare and is probably best avoided. A dark and dingy interior
is also only reserved for the rainiest of days. However, this
vibrant café is a convenient pit-stop for a quick caffeine fix after
an afternoon's shopping and a welcome alternative to Lisbon's
more traditional coffee-houses.

Café Suíça, Praça Dom Pedro IV 96–104, Baixa.
Tel: 21 321 4090
Open: 7am–10pm daily

Sandwiched between the city's busiest two squares, this Lisbon
staple enjoys a central location and constant passing trade.

Tourists flock in their droves to fill the large outdoor terrace on the Rossio, but more seating can be found at the Praça do Figueira entrance on the other side of the building. Great for breakfast and a good spot to watch the daily life of the city unfold. Later in the day, rumbling trams and car exhaust fumes can prove a little excessive. A renovated interior is a mixture of tacky plastic and cheap formica, and has a faceless canteen feel about it. The menu is extensive and boasts a selection of sandwiches, salads, fruit shakes, savoury pastries and cream cakes. A larger dining room offers more substantial meals.

Cerca Moura, Largos das Portas do Sol 4, Graça.
Tel: 21 887 4859
Open: 9am–2am daily

This bar/café is built into the original Moorish city walls after

which it is named. In summer, the esplanade out front is overrun with tourists exploring the hilly backstreets of the Sé. Views of the Alfama and the river are breathtaking on a clear sunny day. The bar serves a selection of savoury snacks and toasted sandwiches well into the night, but outdoor seating is cleared away early if the weather turns. A cave-like interior affords warmth and comfort in the winter months, but low ceilings can be claustrophobic at busy times. Although the combination of bare stone walls and animal print furnishings would look more appropriate in an episode of the Flintstones, it remains cosy and atmospheric.

Confeitaria Nacional, Praça da Figueira 18b/c, Baixa.
Tel: 21 342 4470
Open: 8am–8pm Monday–Friday; 8am–2pm Saturday.
Closed Sunday.

Although this traditional *pasteleria* in the heart of Baixa was founded in 1829, little has changed. It was here that the recipe for

the traditional *bola rei* Christmas cake was first introduced by the French. Cream-painted panelling and a mirrored ceiling make for a lighter ambience than in other more traditional and austere coffee houses. Coloured sweets fill glass jars and a selection of biscuits, cakes and *salgados* are served from the original glass counter. The range is appetizing, but nothing to write home about. Cakes are often sticky and veer on the heavy side. Arrive early to get the best baked produce. A sit-down area is available next door, although service can be frustratingly slow. Given its central location, the place can be overrun with tourists, but locals continue to stop by for a quick *bica* on an afternoon's shopping trip.

Crazy Nuts, Rua Artilharia Um 26, Rato.
Tel: 21 388 3088
Open: noon–3pm, 7pm–midnight. Closed Saturday–Sunday lunch.

If you're grabbed by the sudden desire to devour a burger or sink a frothy milkshake, head to this uptown diner. Crazy Nuts proudly presents itself as Lisbon's first hamburger house – the food is fast and service comes with a smile. The walls are cluttered with Hollywood postcards and 1950s memorabilia assembled in the 20 years since opening. The zebra-print upholstery and collection of inflatable animals hint at the eccentric tastes of crazy owner Carolina, whose larger-than-life presence is most definitely felt. Unfortunately the food isn't quite so impressive,

but being in such good company it's not a problem. Groups of students in thrift-shop threads huddle in the wooden booths, imagining themselves as extras in *American Graffiti*. Hardly Manhattan, but it beats McDonald's any day!

Cultura do Cha, Rua dos Salgadeiras 38, Bairro Alto.
Tel: 21 343 0272
Open: 10am–9.30pm. Closed Sunday.

If tea is your tipple, then Cultura do Cha could be the watering-hole of choice. With 29 different infusions on the menu, it's a mecca of hot beverages. The softly lit interior is warmly enticing and an instant remedy for hangovers. The heavy wooden tables and brightly painted chairs are perfect for a natter, while porcelain teapots complete the comfort. The home-made cakes and delicate pastries that fill the glass cabinets are difficult to resist. Those suffering excesses of the night before should opt for the thickly layered slabs of cheese on toast. The café comes into its own on a rainy Saturday afternoon, when creature comforts are the main priority.

Esplanada, Jardim do Principe Real, Bairro Alto.
Tel: 96 511 5851
Open: 8am–midnight daily

Having opened to a flurry of respectable reviews, this modern café enjoys a peaceful position in the leafy gardens of Príncipe Real. The snaking space-age building looks like a cross between a metal worm tunnel and a flexible vacuum attachment. Laid directly over cobbled paving, it looks deceptively flimsy. On a bright day, the mainly glass structure captures the glorious mid-morning sun and is a perfect choice for a late breakfast. When it pours, the comfy orange armchairs serve as the perfect vantage-point for watching rain hammer against the window panes. Workers from the local interior design community occupy tables during lunchtimes, while a much younger crowd nurse an after-noon coffee at one of the many picnic benches outside. A place to meet and talk the hind leg off a *galao*.

Esplanada da Graça, Largo da Graça.
Open: 10.30am–3am daily (but shorter hours in winter)

There is no shortage of breathtaking *miradouros* in Lisbon, but this particular spot is favoured by locals. In truth it's nothing more than a tiny kiosk serving coffee, beers and toasted sand-wiches. But this is definitely the place to be on a sunny Sunday afternoon. A young crowd armed with guitars and conversation meet to relax in the company of strangers. It makes for perfect people-watching; anything from a canoodling couple to a per-forming labrador can be captured in a 180° glance. Stop for long enough, and you're likely to be engrossed by some activity or another. It's easy to while away the weekend. The cast-iron bells

of the neighbouring church are the only reminder of the hours slipping away.

Esplanada do Adamastor, Largo do Adamastor, Santa Catarina.
Open: 10am–4am daily

Students, travellers and bohemian types frequently gather at this city centre *miradouro* on a sunny afternoon. The café itself is nothing more than a wooden kiosk with limited outdoor seating, but a consistently interesting crowd creates a vibrant buzz. From local estate kids to left-of-centre tourists, it's certainly varied. The spot takes its name from a stone statue of a mythological figure that looms over the space. So laid back it's almost horizontal, the outcrop is a safe haven for cannabis smokers and the smell of hash hangs permanently in the air. The temptation to kick back, relax and admire the stunning view is far too strong to resist.

Martinho da Arcada, Praça do Comercio 3, Baixa.
Tel: 21 887 9259
Open: 7am–10pm. Closed Sunday.

Tucked away in the corner of Praça do Comercio, this traditional tea house opened in 1782. The wood-panelled and white-tiled interior features an image of Fernando Pessoa, who adopted the

139

place as one of his favourite haunts. Once a gambling den, the café now attracts politicians from the surrounding government buildings. It's also a popular pit-stop for commuters on their way to the ferry terminal. The stand-up bar is often busy at lunchtimes and a far more leisurely cup of coffee can be taken at one of the outdoor tables beneath the stone archways. Surprisingly, the hordes of tourists who plague Café Brasíliera and Café Bernard are yet to descend on this peaceful spot. An adjoining restaurant offers finer dining in more stuffy surroundings.

O Cha da Lapa, Rua do Olival 8–10, Lapa.
Tel: 21 390 0888
Open: 9am–8pm daily

This dedicated tea emporium in the wealthy Lapa district caters for finely attired women who continue to make an occasion of an afternoon cuppa. Ornate light-fittings and Regency-inspired gilt furnishings try to emulate the *salon da cha* tradition of the late 1940s. Well-to-do types purse their rouge-red lips and engage in hushed genteel conversation. Unfortunately the tea selection isn't particularly impressive – expect to sip Liptons from fine bone china – and import status stamps a higher price tag. Instead opt for one of the expertly crafted pastries and cream cakes, made daily on the premises. The pleasantly bumbling waiter is as much a reassuring staple as the multi-tiered cake stand in the corner and is more than happy to advise. The building receives very little light,

and is probably best visited on a rainy day.

O Outra Face da Lua, Rua do Norte 86, Bairro Alto.
Tel: 21 343 1631
Open: 3pm–midnight. Closed Sunday.

Not a bar as such, but the tea room annex to this retro clothes store attracts a crowd of self-consciously trendy regulars. Not a drop of alcohol can be found on the premises, but customers find an alternative way to get high: a selection of herbal teas from Holland. A choice of psychedelic infusions boasts properties ranging from calming to energizing, with slightly more punch than your standard PG Tips. Thankfully the neon new-age hippie connotations end there. Music is low-key and surround-

ings relaxed. Funky scene-setters with angular haircuts lounge on orange leather seating behind dividers the colour of boiled sweets. The owner's pet cat has become quite a fixture – it wanders the store with ease and can be found bathing under one of the many neon floor lamps. This is the perfect spot to chill, *and* purchase a vintage Nike tracksuit.

Pão de Canela, Praça das Flores 25–27, Madragoa.
Tel: 21 397 2220
Open: 7.30am–8pm Monday–Friday; 8am–8pm Saturday–Sunday

This popular tearoom and restaurant is named after the cinnamon stick – the ubiquitous coffee-table condiment used by Lisboetas to sweeten a bitter *bica*. Large round tables and pine dressers filled with crockery attract a tastefully dressed middle-class crowd in search of a relaxed breakfast that extends beyond cakes and pastries. Conversation is civilized and the service friendly. Stylish ladies who lunch discuss Gucci glasses and Prada handbags over a *choux* pastry, while at weekends young families settle down for a spot of brunch. This is one of the very few spots open on a Sunday. Overlooking the leafy and peaceful Praça das Flores, the decked outdoor terrace fills up quickly. Unfortunately it's completely shrouded in shade, but a lack of sunlight does little to detract from this *bijou* venue's homely warmth. An adjoining restaurant opens in the evening when the café has closed.

Pasteis de Cerveja, Rua de Belém 15–17, Belém.
Tel: 21 363 4338
Open: 7am–11pm daily

Local converts and curious tourists come to sample this curious
speciality: a sweet pastry made with beer. According to the pro-
prietor, the unique cakes first appeared in the 1920s and have
been popular ever since. The small pies seem to sell like hot
cakes, although in truth the taste of beer is masked by a sweet
almond paste and the novelty value far outweighs the quality of
taste. The café itself is instantly forgettable – a painfully bright
room filled with plastic tables. However, the cakes are sold
exclusively on the premises, giving the owners a comfortable
monopoly. If you can't get enough of the stuff, cardboard carry
cases are available for home delivery. Not the most mouth-

watering of pastries, but an inspired excuse to indulge a sweet
tooth.

Pastelaria Versailles, Avenida Republica 15a, Saldanha.
Tel: 21 354 6340
Open: 7.30am–10pm daily

Easily the best and most traditional of Lisbon's classic tearooms,
Versailles is fortunate enough to escape the obligatory troupes
of tourists that usually follow suit. This is largely a consequence
of its uptown location. Instead, the carved wooden tables are

filled with well-to-do pensioners who chatter in hushed tones over a game of cards. The interior is spectacular: engraved mirrors, stained glass and carved wooden panels. Crystal chandeliers dazzle above the mouth-watering cake cabinet, which seems to stretch into infinity. The daily specials, served with a generous helping of cream, usually disappear quickly. Friendly staff bring a sense of warmth and closeness to this otherwise grand space. Don't leave Lisbon without a visit.

● **Pastelaria-Padaria São Roque, Rua Dom Pedro V 57, Bairro Alto.**
Open: 7am–7.30pm. Closed Sunday.

This 'cathedral of bread' (as proclaimed by *azulejos* behind the

counter) is essentially a bakery, although ample seating is provided for customers who prefer to stay longer. Cakes are sticky and predictably stodgy. But the decoration alone makes this worth a visit. Marble pillars reach into a magnificent dome ceiling. Tiles intricately painted with scenes from nature flood the room with colour. Staff understand little English and territorial locals are somewhat put out by large groups of tourists. This is a real slice of local life.

SV Café, Rua Capelo 20–22, Chiado.
Tel: 21 347 0681
Open: 9.30am–8pm Monday–Wednesday;
9.30am–10pm Thursday–Saturday. Closed Sunday.

Host to regular artistic events and poetry readings this refreshingly modern café is a frequent hub of activity. A young crowd of casual intellectuals and understated creatives regularly drop by for an espresso or a freshly made *salgado*. Snacks and light meals are healthy but varied, and a welcome alternative to the usual deep-fried fare. On Thursday evenings the café also opens for dinners, providing a rotation of themed international dishes. Concealed behind a green and white awning at the bottom of Chiado, SV is close to the area's many boutiques. The space is small and friendly, but yet to develop a strong identity. Colourful artworks brighten the bare brick walls, but are nothing spectacular. A great place for a convenient coffee, but not a destination in itself.

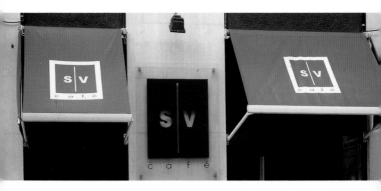

Teatro Taborda, Rua Costa do Castelo 75, Graça.
Tel: 21 887 9484 http://cafe-taborda.planetaclix.pt
Open: 2pm–1am. Closed Monday.

Used primarily by visitors to the Teatro Taborda, this pleasant café is worth a visit in its own right. Located at the quieter end of Costa do Castelo, an inconspicuous entrance betrays none of the activity below. A long rectangular room filled with wooden tables and chairs is reached via a staircase from the theatre. The decoration is simple: there are black and white stills of theatre performances, but the wall-to-wall windows afford a far more dramatic view of the city below. This hilltop retreat is a popular choice for covert liaisons and thoughtful contemplation. You can also get to the shaded outdoor seating area by a path snaking up from Graça. A simple menu of salads and light dishes is served and the bar benefits from a drinks licence. As you'd expect, budding thespians and intellectuals form the bulk of regulars, with the odd circus performer making an appearance!

Verde Perto, Rua Costa do Castelo 26–26a, Alfama.
Tel: 91 830 1020
Open: 11am–7pm (2am Friday, Saturday). Closed Monday.

At first glance it could be mistaken for a contemporary art gallery, but this modern café offers a selection of beverages

(including alcoholic drinks) and a light lunch menu. Owners Iete
Zuzarte and Roland Altmann use the long rectangular glass cabinets to exhibit the jewellery they design, which also happens to
be for sale. The pieces are made from polished stones, mainly
amber and aquamarine, and range from €20 to €1,000. Although
pleasing to the eye, the clean-cut angles and bleached out lighting
can prove slightly disconcerting. Heavy wooden doors open out
onto the street, but on a sunny day Bar des Imagens opposite
proves far more popular. Lunchtime trade is consistent, but this
artistic venture is yet to build a regular crowd. Most custom
comes from middle-class tourists seeking a coffee after visiting
the São Jorge castle.

party...

A typical night out might start in the bars of Bairro Alto, but it rarely ends come last orders. Although there are only a select few venues to choose from, the Lisbon club scene is reliably active. Easily the best choice in Lisbon (and arguably Europe) is Lux; a habourside superclub part-owned by style guru Manuel Reis and Hollywood actor John Malkovich. It's an established favourite with the international DJ set, but the club is somewhat frustratingly fixated with following London fashions – namely the rapid ascendance of electroclash. Every club in Lisbon claims to emulate the style trend set by Lux, but only Op Art manages to do so with success. Less edgy venues follow a loose music policy of commercial crowd-pleasers (Docks, Queens, BBC) and the inevitable high-street house (Kapital, O2Lx). Recently, promoters have started to put on one-off events around the city. Look out for flyers in record shops such as Kingsize Records (Rua da Alfandega 114) or Flur (Avenida Infante Dom Henrique Armazém B).

Most revellers tend to flit between several clubs in one evening, planning their path not by music policy but by virtue of which club will still be open. Most start their night at 2–3am and finish at an after-hours (Paradise Garage, for instance) mid-afternoon the following day. Few clubs are exclusive to one set; utterly incongruous groups of people can pass through the same doors at dif-

ferent times of the night. Lisbon's club scene is sustained by a drugs culture, although few places will tolerate drug use on the premises. Dealers prefer to linger in dark doorways around the Rua dos Poiais de São Bento. Hash resin is openly foisted onto tourists in Praça da Figueira, although it is still considered illegal.

One strange phenomenon is that of the club doormen, who occupy an unparalleled social station in the club scene. They exert full control over the club guest list and have the power to make or break a night. As a result, they are some of the most socially influential people in the city. Another antiquated '80s trend still doing the rounds is the infamous 'ladies' night'. With proper planning, a woman can go out every night without spending a penny!

Portugal's one-time colonial presence continues to be felt in a vibrant African music scene, with visiting artists from Angola, Cape Verde and Guinea Bissau. The best places to sample these sounds are B. Leza and Lontra, with occasional gigs taking place at Net Jazz.

Portugal's indigenous music is the famous *fado*, a melancholic folk song very similar to the blues. Typically associated with the lower classes, *fado* is experiencing a revival and can be heard in a variety of venues – from authentic taverns in the Alfama to fine dining restaurants in Lapa (Senhor Vinho). Inflated minimum charges and hordes of camera-happy tourists are the main drawbacks.

Most strip-clubs in Lisbon are either exceptionally sleazy joints or covert undercover operations. Only a couple are of discernable quality. A row of seedy bars run along Cais do Sodré, while high-class professional pick-up bars cluster around Avenida Duque de Loulé, Elefante Branco being the most well known. Intendente is an overtly red-light district, and a dangerous place for tourists at night. Prostitutes also cruise the empty forest roads of Monsanto.

NIGHTCLUBS

BBC, Avenida Brasília Pavilhão Poente, Alcântara.
Tel: 21 362 4232 www.belembarcafe.com
Open: noon–3pm, 8pm–4am. Closed Sunday.

Encompassing a restaurant, bar and club, this dockside venue is a one-stop shop for an evening out. It's a hot ticket for a wealthy mainstream crowd who demand a high degree of sophistication. The mood is subdued while dinner is served, but come midnight tables and chairs are cleared aside to make way for a dance-floor. The 9-to-5 office crowd who religiously return consider BBC a more accessible alternative to Lux. The fashion crowd would beg to differ. Treading an already safely worn path, trends are followed rather than set. A 'smart shoes' door policy applies, so no trainers are allowed. During the early evening, the water-side tables are a good spot for a cocktail.

B. Leza, Largo Conde Barão 50–52, Cais de Sodré.
Tel: 21 396 3735
Open: 11.30pm–4.30am. Closed Sunday.

This famous music hall is named after one of Cape Verde's biggest producers, whose son happens to own the premises; the name is also a play on the Portuguese word for 'dance'. Key players from the region's music scene regularly perform in this extraordinary

venue. Now worn and crumbling, this former 16th-century palace is nonetheless stunning. Cabaret tables fill the lively main room, which despite its size has the feel of a smoky jazz den. An outdoor courtyard filled with plants offers cool relief on a summer's night. A cheek-to-cheek dance system operates on the dancefloor, so expect to get up close and personal with strangers. A single woman is likely to attract more attention than she bargained for, but pestering men are for the most part harmless. Most fascinating is the Shirley Valentine syndrome so prevalent in the club; frustrated middle-aged housewives make a beeline for nubile African boys. Wonderful on all levels.

Convento, Rua das Escadinhas da Praia 5, Santos.
Tel: 21 395 7101
Open: midnight–4am Friday–Saturday

Essentially a second room to Kremlin, Convento is accessed via a separate entrance (although once inside it's possible to move between both clubs). Fashioned in the style of a church, a giant god-like statue looms over the DJ decks. It's an obvious cliché, but one the clubbers nurture by working themselves into a religious fervour every Saturday night. Both the mood and music are lighter than Kremlin. A friendly gay crowd dominates and not a body in the building is left with a shirt by the end of the night. More musically discerning than most clubs in the city (which can be pretty clueless), it's a recommended dance diva's heaven.

Docks Club, Rua de Cintura Porto de Lisboa 226, Santos.
Tel: 21 395 5875
Open: 11.30pm–6am. Closed Sunday and Monday.

The first club to open on this dockland stretch during the mid-1990s, Docks is yet to pass its peak. Catering for all crowds, from poor-of-pocket students to local wheeler-dealers, it's a no-nonsense party affair. The music policy is whatever sells and the culture of DJ worship is notably absent. There's only one objective for the evening and that's to knock back as many alcopops as is humanly possible. Docks is certainly cheesy, but unlike many other clubs in the city does not have aspirations beyond its station: no hassle, no attitude and certainly no frills.

Incógnito, Rua dos Poiais de São Bento 37, São Bento.
Tel: 21 390 8755 www.incognitobar.com
Open: 11pm–4am. Closed Sunday–Tuesday.

Having recently celebrated its 15th birthday, Incognito is a founding peg in Lisbon's night scene – although these days it functions as a prop rather than a support. Along with Fragil, it was part of a new wave of bars providing an alternative to the traditional *fado* houses. In the halcyon days of the late 1980s, the music policy was one of indie, alt-pop and techno. Little has changed since. Even the moustachioed doorman is a regular fixture. It's a popular choice for students, who flock midweek to hear songs of yes-

teryear. A less than salubrious location necessitates a doorbell policy, but the club is open to all. It's busiest at 2.30am and provides a friendly alternative to the waterfront superclubs.

Kapital, Avenida 24 de Julho 68, Santos.
Tel: 21 395 7101
Open: 10.30pm–6am. Closed Sunday–Monday.

Known to most as a rich man's club, Kapital has catered for Lisbon's jet-set elite since the early 1990s. As with many clubs in the city, change has been slow. Twelve years on, bouncers in full dinner dress look somewhat awkward and ridiculous. But they still hold a position of power equal to the head of state. The club

continues to operate an antiquated three-tier dance-floor system: the ground is a disco (in the broadest sense), the middle a mainstream dance-floor and the top a VIP lounge. The last is a holy grail and desperate pretenders will do anything to climb the social ladder and get in. Filled with more floor cushions than a sheik's harem (and just as many fawning females), it's certainly a pleasant space. Unfortunately, the grey brigade of ministers and businessmen who attend are far less interesting. The club boasts a 'beautiful people' door policy, although in reality it's a haunt for has-beens.

Kremlin, Rua das Escadinhas da Praia 5, Santos.
Tel: 21 395 7101 www.kremlin.pt
Open: midnight–8am (10am). Closed Sunday–Monday.

Love it or hate it (and most Lisboetas learn to love it), Kremlin is an institution in Lisbon's nightlife. The oldest of the city's superclubs, it opened with a fanfare of international DJs and was included by *DJ* magazine in its top 10 clubs in Europe. Twelve years later the heavyweight line-ups have been replaced by an even heavier drug problem… and the odd shooting. However, the benefit of a late licence (most clubs close at 6am) makes Kremlin the perfect venue to witness the multiple cross-sections of Lisbon's social scene collide. Referred to by locals as a 'people zoo', at one time the club was filled with a pantomime of characters; ice-laden pimps would prop up the bar with a high-class

whore on each arm only yards away from well-to-do business-men and immaculately turned-out trendsetters. These days the clientele is much less colourful and far more unsavoury. Strict club etiquette applies at all times; always smile and don't step on anyone's toes. Perfect for people-watching... well, from a distance.

Lontra, Rua de Sao Bento 157, Estrêla.
Tel: 21 396 1083
Open: 10pm–4am. Closed Monday.

Built on the site of a former brothel, this recently reopened club now harbours less seedy activities. It's known primarily as an African club, and the décor is themed accordingly with animal prints, drums and native artefacts spread about the room. Bands

from Cape Verde, Guinea Bissau and other ex-colonies (who still have a strong presence in the city) perform in the main room and regularly bring the house down. The Journeys DJ collective also hosts a popular night on Thursdays. Less intimidating than most African clubs, the appeal is broad-ranging but the mood is always upbeat. Arrive fashionably late to find the party in full swing.

Lux, Avenida Infante Dom Henrique, Santa Apolónia.
Tel: 21 882 0890 www.luxfragil.com
Open: 10pm–6am Tuesday–Saturday

Easily the trendiest club in Lisbon, and contender for the European title, Lux has redefined the city's club scene since opening in 1998. It's complemented by Bica do Sapato and a string of design shops, making this dockside strip a trendsetter's heaven. When Manuel Reis (the man behind the legendary Fragil) chose to build a development on the derelict Santa Apolonia dock, few believed it would be so successful. In terms of shell and soul, Lux is yet to be rivalled. A spacious square dance-floor is interrupted only by crisp white pillars; giant glitterballs are a nod to New York's Studio 54. A balcony overlooking the river runs around the club and is popular in the early hours. The club attracts beautiful *glitterati*, larger-than-life drag queens and Bairro Altistas, although there have been complaints that the encroach-ment of an affluent jet-set has lowered the tone. Security is tight and the club runs a strict anti-drugs policy – bouncers roaming

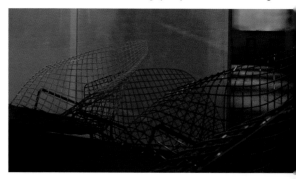

the dance-floor can be disconcerting at times. Door staff are also a victim of their own hype. International DJs visit regularly and attract long queues. The music policy tends to follow London's lead.

O2Lx, Cais Rocha Conde de Óbidos, Armazém 113, Lapa.
Tel: 21 393 2520
Open: midnight–6am Wednesday–Saturday

As close to a Euro-club stereotype as you can can get, 02Lx is

the place to throw shapes on a Saturday night. Music is hard, fast and drug-inspired. Exposed metal walkways and thick steel pillars have industrial connotations that are a frightening throwback to discotheques of the 1980s. A mid-30 crowd arrives in soft-top convertibles, left abandoned in the driveway. Once inside, businesswomen in Chanel suits and men in Pringle sweaters splash vast wads of cash at the bar. In the main room, a predominantly gay crowd bathe bare-chested in the lurid neon lasers. Hands aloft, they work themselves into a near-euphoric trance. A quite literally star-studded staircase leads to an out-of-bounds VIP area, to which desperate hordes clamber to gain access. Attitude is everything; believe your own hype and so will everyone else.

Unlike the many faceless and identikit bars that line the Doca de Santo Amaro, Op Art benefits from a trend-setting crowd of discerning clubbers. The square-shaped building stands alone as a pocket of cool in a largely characterless area. A music policy of electro and house emulates London trends, and many regard the place as a miniature Lux. During the day customers come to enjoy a coffee on the outdoor esplanade, overshadowed only by the Ponte 25 de Abril suspension bridge. The kitchen serves a selection of steaks, salads and fish until 11.30pm. By night slip mats replace saucers and the space quickly fills with music-hungry revellers. The busiest times are the early hours when many other clubs have closed. Outdoor seating provides a welcome breath of fresh air, but the structural glass walls can be uncomfortable at daybreak. Bright shards of sunlight are guaranteed to clear even the foggiest of beer goggles. If you prefer to party in the dark, steer well clear. But there's no better place to watch the sun rise during the height of summer.

Paradise Garage, Rua João Oliveira Miguéis 38–48, Alcântara.
Tel: 21 324 3400 www.paradisegarage.com
Open: 10.30pm–4am Thursday–Saturday; after hours, 10am–4pm Sunday

There are many faces to this warehouse conversion located beneath a flyover. During the week it's a lively music venue where local and foreign rock bands play to a young crowd. At weekends it's a popular choice for under-age drinkers who congregate in groups outside. But the club comes into its own on a Sunday morning, when those who refuse to go home take advantage of the after-hours opening. It's the final leg in the weekend marathon for most clubbers, and not for the faint-hearted. But for many the laid-back music (garage, funnily enough) puts a comfortable lid on the night. Some revellers choose to stay in on a Saturday night and turn up straight after a bowl of cornflakes. It's difficult to say which sight is more disconcerting! Popular simply because there is simply nowhere else to go at that time of the morning. Dark glasses are obligatory.

People, Rua do Instituto Industrial 6, Santos.
Tel: 21 396 4841 www.people.pt
Open: midnight–6am Thursday–Saturday

Clubs are often a momentary expression on the changing face of Lisbon's nightlife, but the opening of People last year was embraced with much interest. The venue, a former factory, had been home to popular club, Industria, and regarded by many as a great space. A year after it closed, Sofia Cunha e Silva and her sister decided to start up another club here – a brave venture in a scene largely dominated by balding males. After a spell of research in the world's top international club world, the girls have settled on a 'happy house' policy for the new place, akin to the New York gay house scene of the early 1990s. Sofia, who was formerly doing PR work for elite club Kapital, hopes to use her clientele database to attract a crowd of rich *fashionistas* and

beautiful faces. In reality the club lies somewhere between a slightly more up-market Docks and a vastly less fashionable Lux. Nevertheless, People at least goes some way to bridge the cavernous void between the extremes of Lisbon's nightlife.

Queens, Rua da Cintura do Porto (Avenida Brasília) Armazém H, Santos.
Tel: 21 395 5870
Open: 10pm–6am Wednesday–Saturday

Once a gay hang-out, this warehouse club is now popular with a marginally less decadent and considerably less interesting crowd. Still, it's a better option than most bargain-basement clubs on the *docas* strip. Neon inflatables suspended from the ceiling and *faux*-flame candles are deliciously tacky; the mock-Hawaiian beach bar out back is even more entertaining. But you can't knock Queens – it certainly aims to please the masses, who jostle for space on the sweaty dance-floor. Ladies' night (every Wednesday) proves most popular. It's a hot choice for businessmen in casual dress, intent on wooing their fawning secretaries.

W, Rua Maria Luísa Holstein 13, Alcântara.
Tel: 21 363 6830
Open: 10pm–6am Wednesday and Sunday

The steel-framed doors that form the back-alley entrance to this club can be slightly disconcerting; the over-oiled and super-slick doormen are even more unwelcoming. But, rest assured, once inside the mood is much lighter. Large steel pillars and soft ceiling lights provide ample seclusion, while leather sofas can be occupied for hours on end. The music veers from R&B to pop house, along with the age range of customers. Expect a road-block on Wednesdays, when groups of over-styled and under-dressed teenage girls take advantage of ladies' night. Gentlemen can expect to pay anything up to €30 – there's no equality of the

sexes here! Many, salivating on arrival, are happy to part with their cash. The real party takes place on a Sunday night, when the club opens specially for other workers in the nightlife sector unable to let loose on any other night.

MUSIC CLUBS

Clube de Fado, Rua São João a Praça 92–94, Alfama.
Tel: 21 888 2694
Open: 7pm–2am daily

Owned by *fado* guitarist Mario Pacheco, this atmospheric club is a relative newcomer to the scene. The architecture, however, is far more ancient, with stone columns, arches and a Moorish well. Nestled beneath the tranquil Se cathedral, it's a lovely location. Traditional *fadistas* such as Maria Armanda, Dr Fernando, Machado Soares and Maria da Nazare play alongside younger faces such as José da Camara and Paulo Braganca. Artists perform between courses in an intimate dining room, but an upstairs gallery can be used by those who just want to drink. Food is heavy, traditional and – like most *fado* clubs – expensive.

Hot Clube, Praça da Alegria 39, Restauradores.
Tel: 21 346 7369 www.hcp.pt
Open: 10pm–2am Tuesday–Saturday (live music starts 11pm). Closed Sunday–Monday.

Faded posters of Miles Davis and original billboards of seminal jazz festivals proudly adorn the walls of Lisbon's oldest and most famous jazz bar. Underground in the truest sense of the word, Hot Clube is more a den than a club house. Low ceilings and a smoky atmosphere are certainly authentic, but cramped and uncomfortable when more than 50 people turn up. A back patio catches some overspill. Hot Clube has built on a solid reputation

over the years, and the standard of classic jazz is always high. Many big-name artists drop by for an impromptu jam after playing bigger venues. The place is dripping with nostalgia, but with good reason.

Senhor Vinho, Rua do Meio a Lapa 18, Lapa.
Tel: 21 397 7456
Open: 8pm–1.30am (shows start at 9.30pm). Closed Sunday.

The most reputable, and accordingly expensive, of Lisbon's *fado* houses, Senhor Vinho is owned by the world-famous singer Maria Da Fé. Occasionally Maria takes to the dining floor, but more often the overtly sweet but painfully tragic tones of rising star Mariza can be heard. Seven different singers perform in rotation basis at 20-minute intervals during the course of the evening. The food served is excellent, but tables are filled quickly. Opened in 1975, the building was once a bakery and the giant brick oven is now a waiting area for artists preparing to per-

form. Although large tour groups form the bulk of guests, Senhor Vinho has maintained a proud sense of sophistication. As up-market as *fado* gets.

Speakeasy, Cais das Oficinas, Rocha Conde d'Óbidos, Armazém 115.
Tel: 21 395 7308
Open: 10pm–4am Monday–Saturday (live music starts at 10.30pm)

Jazz purists tend to turn their nose up at this more mainstream music bar. Straddling a broad divide between traditional jazz and palatable middle-of-the-road, the music is subsequently diluted. But it's enough to keep a heaving crowd happy. Expect to hear

jazz, funk and blues regularly with occasional, more heavily promoted events. Early evening steak and chips are served at candlelit wooden tables, but arrive late and it's standing-room only. The wealthy jet-set that cruises this dockland stretch has taken to using the bar as a post-dinner mid-week port of call. The bar is owned by the sons of *fado* singer Carlos do Carmo.

ADULT ENTERTAINMENT

Champagne Club, Rocha Conde d'Óbidos, Armazém 115
Tel: 21 396 1886 www.champagne-club.com
Open: 10pm–4am daily

The first table dance club to open in Lisbon, Champagne is a welcome alternative to the seedy old-fashioned strip-joints that

populate the city. It's run along the lines of an American strip-bar, and shows are topless only. Unlike other bars, the club is selective when it comes to clientele, and the girls treated as professionals. Expect to see 10–12 different performers over the course of one night hailing from Portugal, Holland, Canada and Eastern Europe, with regular 'star' appearances by US *Playboy* models. Drinks cost around €10, while a table dance will set you back €30 (which includes two drinks); the entrance fee is €25. The venue itself is stunning: a wall-to-ceiling single-way window commands breathtaking views of the Tejo at night. A high-tech light show and comfortable surroundings meet with the approval of Lisbon's moneyed elite. A secure environment enjoyed by both men and women.

Savana Club, Rua Borges Carneiro 38, Lapa.
Tel: 21 390 2141
Open: 11pm–4.30am. Closed Sunday.

Less glamorous than Champagne, but still reasonably reputable, this intimate strip-club is favoured by stag groups. Entrance costs €25 (including a drink) and shows start at midnight. Two side rooms are reserved for private dances (€40) while a table dance

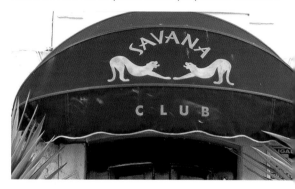

costs €25. Eight girls work the club and are a mixture of Portuguese, Brazilian, Russian and Eastern European. The club is simple, but tasteful and comfortably dark without being dingy. Door staff are also relaxed and friendly. The club benefits from an inconspicuous location in the quiet backstreets of Lapa. Interestingly enough, the current PM's house lies opposite.

Show Girls, Avenida Almirante gago Coutinho (just before the airport).
Tel: 21 853 2428
Open: 10pm–4am Monday–Wednesday; 10pm–5am Thursday–Saturday

More novelty than quality entertainment, this overtly kitsch strip-bar beggars belief. It's actually housed in an abandoned aeroplane, *en route* to the city airport. Ask any taxi driver and they'll know what you're talking about; the club has become

something of a national landmark. Rather amusingly, lap dances take place in the cockpit. By no standards is this a high-class affair, but drunken groups of tourists seem to find the concept incredibly entertaining.

culture...

Relative to many of its European counterparts, Portugal has been somewhat unfairly considered a cultural pauper – in marked contrast to its former wealth of empire, once stretching from Brazil to Macau. Cultural development was hampered for several reasons: the disabling earthquake of 1755, a long-running quasi-fascist dictatorship until 1974 and a lack of economic investment.

Today all that is starting to change. Events such as the colossal Experimenta Design Biennale exhibition and the building of Parque das Nações for Expo '98 signify a fresh emphasis on artistic pursuits.

Although many dance and music repertoires are classical, new auditoriums such as the CCB and Teatro Luís de Camões have given performances a lease of new life. Two key historical theatres are still active in Lisbon: the Teatro Dona Maria Nacional II and the Teatro Nacional de São Carlos.

The Gulbenkian Foundation, with its own orchestra, auditoriums, ballet company and art gallery, remains the most defining contemporary collective.

Lisbon itself is a crumbling museum-piece; church ruins and striking façades bear witness to the city's troubled history. The earliest ruins, underneath the

Castelo de São Jorge, date back to 138 BC and the Roman occupation. The city fell to the Visigoths (in 469) for a brief period before the Moors moved in (in 714) and made their presence felt with a new building on the castle foundations and a *cerca moura* (siege wall) enclosing 15 hectares of the city.

After the Christian re-conquest in 1140, the next great period of cultural development came in 1415 when Henry the Navigator embarked on the Maritime Age of Discoveries, and in 1494 the Treaty of Tordesillas divided the world between Portugal and Spain. Dom Manuel I used riches from the sea routes for

building projects and developed the extravagant form of architecture known as Manueline; the best standing examples are the Torre de Belém and Mosteiro dos Jerónimos. During the 1600s a trend for baroque architecture developed, as did the fashion for *azulejos* (blue and white tiles) which now characterize so many of Lisbon's buildings. An earthquake and accompanying tidal wave in 1755 flattened much of the city and led to the Pombaline reconstruction under the Marquês de Pombal.

Political unrest engulfed Portugal in 1910 with a Republican revolt; during the next 16 years there were 45 different governments until the military finally took over in 1926. A lively culture flourished during the First Republic of 1915: the publication of *Orfeu* magazine introduced poet Fernando Pessoa and painter Jose de Almeida Negreiros. Much of this was stifled by the new regime in 1926. Lisbon's final dictator, Oliveira Salazar, came to power in 1932 and concentrated his efforts on glorifying Portuguese achievements while closing the country off from international influence. The revolution of 1974 finally saw Portugal divest itself of its overseas colonies, and a new age of consumer society dawned.

SIGHTSEEING

Castelo de São Jorge, Castelo.
Tel: 21 887 7244
Open: 9am–9pm, April–September; 9am–6pm, October–March

Situated atop one of Lisbon's seven hills are the ruins of this magnificent castle, originally built by the Visigoths in the 5th century. It was later fortified with a 2km wall by the Moors in the 9th century. In 1147, following the Christian ransacking, it fell to Portugal's first king, Afonso Henriques, whose statue stands beyond the main castle gate. The Palácio de Alcacovas was home to Portuguese royalty for centuries, but when attention turned to the sea in the 17th century, it fell into ruin. Today, the crumbling turrets serve as a romantic backdrop for a sunset stroll. The Olissiponia, an excellent multimedia exhibition, gives a commentary on the city's history. The Camara Escura, a periscope with mirror and two lenses on top of the Tower, reflects 360° images of Lisbon inside. English commentary is available.

Centro de Arte Moderna, Rua Dr. Nicolau de Bettencourt 1050.
Tel: 21 782 3000 www.gulbenkian.pt
Open: 2–6pm Tuesday; 10am–6pm Wednesday–Sunday.
Closed Monday.

Opened in 1983, the Fundação Calouste Gulbenkian's Modern

Art Centre contains the country's largest and finest collection of
20th-century Portuguese art, including pieces from defining artist
Amadeo de Souza Cardosa. An exhibition of British art also
dates from the 1960s. Worthy of mention is Amadeo and
Antonio Areal's interpretation of Picasso's *Les Demoiselles
d'Avignon*, part of Areal's showing at the 9th Sao Paulo Biennial in
1967. The Foundation gardens also contain several sculptures
organized in an art trail, and make for a pleasant summer stroll.
Guided tours in English can be booked. A joint ticket may be
purchased for the neighbouring Gulbenkian Museum, which
houses a mammoth collection of Western and Eastern art.

Convento do Carmo, Largo do Carmo, Chiado.
Tel: 21 346 0473
Open: 10am–5pm. Closed Sunday.

Described as the most beautiful church in Lisbon, only the Gothic arches, walls and flying buttresses are still standing; the roof collapsed on a crowd of worshippers during the 1755 earthquake. It was built in 1423 under the instruction of Nuno Alvares Pereira, Dom João I's military commander, who was unwavering in his choice of location. Metro tunnelling in recent years has also brought the structure to near collapse. Today a grassy lawn grows amid the ruins, which rise boldly against Lisbon's deep blue sky. The back end of the church, with ceiling intact, houses the Museu Arqueologico with its random collection of European and Egyptian antiquities. Afterwards, relax with a coffee in the peaceful Largo do Carmo.

Elevador da Santa Justa, Rua de Aurea, Baixa.
Open: 9am–7pm daily

Possibly the best and fastest way to see Lisbon, this 45m-high wrought-iron elevator is one of the city's most distinctive landmarks. Officially opened in 1901, it was designed and built by Eiffel disciple Raul Mesnier de Ponsard. It was originally intended to link the Rua de Aurea with the Largo do Carmo, but the bridging viaduct was closed due to structural problems. The lift is now a tourist attraction with a café atop the metal platform. The 360° panorama is an ideal way to find your bearings in the city. Bus and tram tickets are valid for a ride, although at peak times queues for the lift can be long.

Mãe de Água, Jardim das Amoreiras, Rato.
Tel: 21 325 1646
Open: 10am–6pm. Closed Sunday.

Completed in 1835, the Aquaducto das Águas Livres ('aqueduct of free waters') was built to bring the city its first clean drinking water. The 109 stone arches extend from Lisbon across the hills 18 miles into Canecas. The inaugural stone was laid at the Mãe de Água ('mother of water'), which now stands behind the Socialist Party headquarters on Largo do Rato. The reservoir can hold 5,500 cubic metres of water. The cool stone chamber, with its floating platform, is now used for art exhibitions. Climb onto the roof for a wonderful view of the city. Take a train from Rossio to Campolide to see the aqueduct at its most impressive – 65m high. Enthusiasts should also visit the Museu da Água in a former pumping station on Rua do Aviela 12, Santa Apolonia (tel: 21 813 5522).

Mosteiro dos Jerónimos, Praça do Imperio, Belém.
Tel: 21 362 0034
Open: 10am–1pm, 2–5.30pm Tuesday–Sunday. Closed Monday.

This prime example of Manueline architecture was built on the orders of Dom Manuel I to commemorate the Portuguese discoveries. Monks of the Order of St Jerome were given the spiritual responsibility of comforting and giving guidance to sailors. The tomb of Vasco da Gama lies inside a 25m baroque vault opposite that of poet Louis de Camões. Work on the impressive structure began in 1502, following a design by architect Diogo de Boitaca, and was not completed until towards the end of the 16th century. The sculptural façade features a hierarchical display of saints, topped by patron saint St Mary of Bethlehem (Belém). The tranquil cloisters, designed by Boytac and completed by João de Castilho, are frequently used for theatre performances and concerts. Admission prices apply to the monastery and cloisters, although entry to the church is free.

Museu do Design, Centro Cultural de Belém, Praça do Imperio, Belém.
Tel: 21 361 2400
Open: 11am–8pm daily

Part of the Centro Cultural de Belém, the Design Museum is considered one of the best in Europe. The private collection of innovative furnishings and everyday objects was amassed by media executive Francisco Capelo. Exhibits are divided into three areas – Luxury, Pop and Cool – and arranged chronologically. Oddly, the exhibition starts in 1937, the year of the Paris International Exhibition when, according to Capelo, designers first tackled new materials with a traditional approach. Capelo believed his museum would help promote contemporary design

– a field in which international influence was so restricted in pre-revolutionary years. The museum contains over 600 items from around the world, including stainless-steel sofas, Perspex arm-chairs and metal storage units.

Museu Nacional do Azulejo, Rua da Madre de Deus 4.
Tel: 21 814 7747
Open: 2–6pm Tuesday; 10am–6pm Wednesday–Sunday.
Closed Monday.

Lisbon's ubiquitous trademark *azulejos* are well documented in this museum, which contains tiles from the 15th century onwards as well as some more modern considerations. The building, a former convent of the Igreja de Nossa Senhora da

Madre de Deus, provides an inspiring backdrop. It was founded for the Poor Clare order of nuns in 1509 by Dona Leonor, wife of Dom João II. Highlights include a 36m-long panel depicting Lisbon before the 1755 earthquake, a Manueline cloister and opulent baroque chapel with gilt wood carvings. The courtyard gardens are also a wonderful place to enjoy lunch. The museum is slightly out of town and is best reached by taxi or the 104/105 buses from Praça do Comercio.

Ocenarium, Esplanada Dom Carlos I, Doca Olivais.
Tel: 21 891 7006 www.oceanario.pt
Open: 10am–7pm daily

Second only to the aquarium in Osaka, Lisbon's Oceanario is the main attraction at the former Expo site. Designed by the American specialist architect Peter Chermeyeff, it contains over 25,000 fish, birds and mammals in four different holding tanks representing species from the Antarctic, Indian, Pacific and Atlantic oceans. A large central tank containing all manner of tropical fish and fearsome hammerhead sharks can be viewed from different angles over two storeys. High-tech multi-lingual interactive displays explain the development of ocean life. The glass cube structure is set out on the water, with the spectacular Teleferico (cable car) running overhead. On a clear day the mammoth 11km Ponte Vasco da Gama bridge is visible.

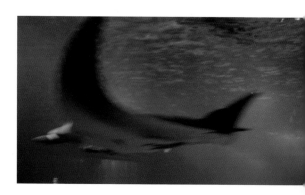

Torre de Belém, Praça da Torre de São Vicente de Belém.
Tel: 21 362 0034
Open: 10am–5pm in winter; 10am–6.30pm in summer

Built on the orders of Dom Manuel the Fortunate, the Torre was intended as a fortress to guard the entrance to Lisbon's harbour. Positioned 1km away from the Mosteiro dos Jerónimos, it originally stood mid-stream while the monastery was on the shoreline. The tide since drifted south and the tower can be reached by a walkway; nothing is more amusing than watching tourists attempt to dodge the incoming waves. Designed by Diogo and Francisco Arruda, the tower is a mixture of early Gothic, Byzantine and Manueline styles. There are stonework motifs of the maritime discoveries and a sculpture of Saint Vincent, the patron saint of Lisbon. A rhinoceros under the north-west watch tower supposedly inspired Durer's drawing of the devil.

THEATRE AND OPERA

Centro Cultural de Belém, Praça do Imperio, Belém.
Tel: 21 361 2400 www.ccb.pt
Open: 8.30am–9.45pm daily (box office)

Boasting Lisbon's largest auditorium, the CCB easily has the city's best facilities. The grey block-like limestone structure, designed by Vittorio Gregotti and Manuel Salgado, caused no end of

controversy when it opened in 1993. Now the CCB plays host to some of the best music, theatre and dance events from both foreign and domestic companies. Several vast exhibition spaces also feature a varied programme of art exhibitions. A cafeteria and open-air concourse are great places to relax.

Chapitô, Costa do Castelo 1.
Tel: 21 887 8225/886 1419 www.chapito.org

Set up by Portugal's first female clown, the Chapitô world comprises a circus school, theatre group, bar, restaurant and various youth projects. The theatre, home to the Companhia de Chapitô, is a small space suited to the group's humorous, physical and confrontational style of performance. Artistic direction is cour-

tesy of John Mowat, of London's Oddbodies theatre group, and shows are in a mixture of English and Portuguese. After the show, share a drink with the cast in a makeshift bar below a colourful tree-house belonging to the school crèche. A unique experience.

Coliseu dos Recreios, Rua das Portas de Santo Antao 96, Baixa.
Tel: 21 324 0580 www.coliseulisboa.com

Lisbon's impressive coliseum was built in 1890, and used as a cir-

cus venue and opera house before turning its charms to a range of modern conventions and classical music events. A variety of gigs and rock concerts take place here. Restoration and remodelling work was undertaken during the early 1990s.

Fundação Calouste Gulbenkian, Rua Dr. Nicolau Bettencourt, Praça de Espanha.
Tel: 21 793 5131 www.gulbenkian.pt
Open: 1–7pm daily (box office)

Ranking alongside the CCB as one of Lisbon's most important cultural venues, the Gulbenkian has its own orchestra, choir and ballet company. Iranian philanthropist and patron of the arts,

Armenian Calouste Gulbenkian bequeathed his wealth to set up this extraordinary foundation in 1955 after finding asylum in Portugal. With over US$1 billion in assets, it has a bigger budget than some Portuguese government ministries. Constituting only 60 members, the Orquestra Gulbenkian sits somewhere between a chamber group and symphony orchestra. A number of international orchestras and chamber groups plays here throughout the year; festivals of contemporary music (May) and early music (October) take place along with regular concerts in the outdoor amphitheatre.

Teatro Nacional de São Carlos, Rua Sepra Pinto 9, Chiado.
Tel: 21 325 3045/6 www.saocarlos.pt
Open: 1–7pm daily (box office)

Inspired by La Scala, Lisbon's main opera house was built in the late 18th century. Today, it is a place for opera, classical music and ballet. Excellent acoustics and a stunning rococo interior regularly wow audiences. The state-run Orquestra Sinfonica Portuguesa is based here. The theatre also organizes the Musica em Novembro festival of contemporary music. Operatic seasons vary and tickets range between €8 and €15.

**Teatro Nacional Dona Maria II, Praça Dom Pedro IV
(Rossio).**
Tel: 21 347 2246

Dating back to the mid-19th century, the columns of Portugal's
national theatre dominate Rossio square. The statue on top of
the façade is Gil Vicente, the father of Portuguese theatre.
Initially intended to help civilize the Portuguese nation, it has
done little in recent years to support contemporary projects.
The Nacional presents a repertoire of Portuguese and foreign
plays, although most performances are in Portuguese. The season
normally runs from autumn to spring.

shop...

Surprisingly for a capital city, Lisbon does not foster a strong shopping culture; most locals are too busy spending money in the city's multitude of cafés and restaurants to pursue material pleasures. That said, most shops are conveniently clustered by genre, making shopping trips a pleasurable breeze rather than a blow to the head.

For a taste of indigenous produce, head to the Baixa. Here many of the city's traditional craft shops continue to serve customers thanks to a freeze on rents and a reluctance to redevelop. Many are worth a visit for their fantastic façades alone, but don't miss the authentic taste of the city's past that's on offer inside. Overflowing with colourful beads and accessories, the haberdasheries and fabric stores are difficult to resist – even if you have absolutely no intention of getting anywhere near a sewing machine.

Downtown Lisbon is a good place to buy leather goods of varying price and quality; shoes come cheap but will not always last the distance. Those wishing to take home a taste of the city in the most literal sense will not be disappointed by the *garrafeiras* (wine merchants) and delis.

Traditional crafts include glassware, ceramics and a trade in the wonderful *azule-*

jos (tiles) that give the façades of Lisbon's buildings their distinctive character; Solar has a fantastic selection of antique tiles and will ship worldwide. Other traditional shops worth a visit are Casa das Vellas Loreto (a candlemaker's, specializing in fragrance and design), Alceste (a perfume house), Ervanaria Rosil (herbalists with an assortment of medicinal teas), Luvaria Ulisses (a glove shop) and the intriguing Hospital das Bonecas (a hospital for dolls). Antiques and knick-knacks can be picked up along the Rua de São Bento, while a number of interior design shops have sprung up around Rato and Principe Real.

A Saturday-afternoon shopping trip is usually conducted in the fashionable Chiado district, where shoppers can flit between exclusive boutiques and their high-street alternatives. A large pedestrian area lends itself to street performance and is a pleasant place to rest between bouts of spending.

For high fashion lines from international labels, head to the Avenida da Liberdade. Home-grown Portuguese fashion is still relatively fledgling, with most young designers based in the backstreets of Bairro Alto. Ana Salazar, the pioneer of Portuguese fashion, launched her own label in the 1980s, paving the way for a plethora of design schools. Despite hosting its own fashion week, Portugal is still struggling for recognition in the world of *haute couture*. Most Lisboetas prefer to do their shopping out of town, and will proudly recommend one of the many new American-style malls to visitors. Although convenient, these largely uninspiring spaces are home to the usual suspects on the high street.

Shops are generally open from 10am to 7pm, although many still close for a long lunch, and the more alternative boutiques (in Bairro Alto) function on a much later body clock.

AVENIDA DA LIBERDADE

The largest road in Lisbon, the Avenida is also home to many of international fashion's biggest names. Even the most hardened of shoppers couldn't fail to run the gauntlet of designer boutiques without exhausting their legs – and wallet. Most high fashion labels are represented, either under their own steam or as a concession in larger stores. The city's hotels are largely concentrated in this area, which has an accordingly cosmopolitan flavour.

Adolfo Dominguez Spanish fashion house specializing in smart cut suits, casuals and accessories

Ayer fashion house stocking make-up and designer collections from Christian Lacroix

Betty Barclay stylish ladies fashion

Carolina Herrera *haute couture* and ready-to-wear lines from New York design guru

David Rosas designer jewellers with lines from Patek Phillipe and Bulgari

Emporio Armani international high fashion, very 1990s

Hugo Boss men's fashion, omnipresent in every European city

LA Lanidor fashion store selling designer concessions

Mango young and affordable Spanish high-street trend

Massimo Dutti basic casuals for men and women from a Spanish designer

Purification Garcia men's and women's classic cut fashions from a Spanish designer

Sacoor Brothers preppy men's and women's clothing

Forum Tivoli

A small shopping mall located on the Avenida.

Champ leather bags from the Parisian Longchamp design house

Fashion Clinic young designer with concessions from Prada, D&G, DK and Miss Sixty

Philosophie contemporary trends and international fashion lines

BAIXA

Traditional traders can still be found in the criss-cross streets of the Baixa. Many have been selling their wares for over 100 years thanks to lease laws enforcing a freeze on rents. A colourful collection of haberdashers, perfumeries, tailors and miracle herbalists can be found crammed into the tiny backstreets. Historically, the roads of the Baixa were named after different trades, which in the case of Rua da Aurea, a street of jewellers, continues to be the case.

Rua Augusto

A Pompadour beauty products and underwear

Archega sophisticated women's knitwear

Augustus Portuguese designer silk and sequinned ladies' evening wear

Bershka young Spanish high-street fashions

Casa Macario selling wines, cigars, ports and teas for 90 years

Charles mid-range fashions, leather and suede boots and bags

Galerias Rivoli traditonal fabric store

Jivago traditional tailors for men

Love fashion store housing designs from CK, DK, Fendi and Guess

Luis Vuitton luxury French fashion house

Mango young high-street fashions from a famous Spanish chain

Nunes Correa former royal tailors selling made-to-measure suits

Often by Pull and Bear smart men's casuals

La Perla slinky Italian lingerie

Zara smart casual wear from this Spanish chain

Zeva designer women's wear with more formal collections

Rua da Prata

Albilini smart women's knitwear

Barbosa Esteves antique and contemporary jewellery

LA Lanidor up-market department store stocking women's designer labels

Malibu smart women's casuals

Rua da Conceição

Alceste old-fashioned perfumery, blending fragrances since 1910

Luis S Fernandes traditional haberdashers offering glamorous furs and fabrics

Rua da Aurea

Aurea specializes in antique brooches

Correira antique jewellery, precious stones and silver

Diadema classic jewellery, watches and silverwear

Luva d'Ouro contemporary jewellery design using beads and enamel

Teixera Bastos antiques and religious effigies

Rua da Betesga

Manuel Tavares deli selling an impressive range of *chourico* (sausage), cheese and port

Rua da Madalena

Ervanaria Rosil tea emporium and herbalist for over 100 years
Santos Oficios Artesanatos hand-made blankets, rugs, pottery and baskets

BAIRRO ALTO

Popular with the alternative fashion set, some of Lisbon's most exciting young designers have set up shop here. Many, however, have equally alternative opening hours. During the day, *'volta ja'* ('back soon') signs are a common sight in shop windows: the area generally comes to life after 5pm. Shopping is a social experience and stores often stay open well into the night. Distinctions of function are also blurred, with shops doubling up as cafés, bars and downsized-clubs.

Rua da Rosa

Aleksander Protich feminine fabrics with quirky detailing from a Belgrade-born designer.

Annette Strootmann contemporary and hand-made knitwear from a German designer using comfortable and imported wools
Espumante Bairrada warehouse of wine and port
Mao Mao young club fashions and retro wear
Moldura do Bairro Alto fine art photography and stencilled tiles
Tereza Seabra jewellery workshop specializing in contemporary designs using beadwork, silver and felt corsage

Rua da Atalaia

Fatima Lopes extrovert fashions from larger-than-life designer; also houses a bar and club
la colourful and distinctive knitwear from Portuguese designer Lena Aires
Mercearia di Atalaia gourmet delicatessen
Sesim Loja funky club jewellery in extravagant designs; also a café

Rua do Norte

Agenzia 117 sexy 1970s-inspired fashions that make a statement
Eldorado colourful funky club-wear from one of Lisbon's original alternative stores
Fake Lisbon trendy retro trainer store with café space
O Outra Face da Lua second-hand and retro-wear; also serves herbal concoctions
Sneakers Delight trainer emporium stocking latest trends

CHIADO

Designer boutiques and high-street favourites sit alongside traditional craftsmen in Lisbon's most popular shopping district. The area underwent a transformation after a devastating fire in 1988, the most recent addition being the Armazens do Chiado shopping centre. There are plenty of good cafés for resting tired feet once you've shopped and dropped. Young teens tend to hang around the Rua Garratt on a Saturday afternoon.

Largo do Chiado

Antonio da Silva antique jewellery from the 18th and 19th centuries

Hermes French fashion house selling bags, watches, clothes and perfume

Lalique high-quality crystal ornaments and jewellery

Vista Alegre fine crystal, crockery and tea sets from famous a Portuguese homeware specialist

Rua do Loreto

Caza das Vellas Loreto a house of candles since 1789; everything is made on the premises

Mayer trader in antique jewellery, cameras and knick-knacks

Rua do Carmo

A Loja do Gato Preto homeware and linens in contemporary designs

Aerosoles fashion shoes specializing in comfort soles

Ana Salazar men's and women's wear from a leading Portuguese fashion designer

Au Bontieur des Dames young fashions from Miss Sixty, Trussarddi and Chevignon

H&M Scandinavian high-street fashions

Luvaria Ulisses gloves in all shapes, sizes and materials

Marallo Italian designer women's footwear

Osklen youth fashions from this Brazilian high-street store

Perfumes e Companhia perfume department store
Tommy Hilfiger young casual fashions from American designer
Women's Secret stylish women's underwear

Rua Garrett

Benetton young Italian high-street fashion chain
Bershka young high-street Spanish fashions
Bertrand Liveiros Lisbon's oldest bookshop
Cartier French watchmakers and luxury jewellers
Casa Pereira established shop selling imported coffee from the ex-colonies
Fun and Basics fashion handbags, jewellery, bags and belts
House of Villeroy and Boch crockery and kitchenware since 1748
Nespresso designer coffee equipment from Krups and Nespresso
Ourivesaria Alianca elaborate jewellers decorated in the style of Louis XV, selling trinkets and pendents
Paris Em Lisboa old-fashioned department store housing contemporary household designs
Sousa smart evening wear and fabrics

SANTA APOLONIA

Avenida Infante Dom Henrique Armazém B

The work of style-genius Manuel Reis, this designer dockside development plays host to a select number of cutting-edge shops. Most are open late and are worth a browse before a meal at Bica do Saparto.

Flur DJ-friendly record shop selling an impressive dance music selection

Lojad Atalaia furniture in extravagant modern designs, owned by Manuel Reis; formerly in Rua da Atalaia in Bairro Alto

Nord Scandinavian design shop

Sneakers Delight larger branch of Bairro Alto's trend trainer store

SÃO BENTO/RATO

With more antique stores than any other street in Lisbon (or Portugal), Rua de São Bento is the place to come for an original

19th-century exotic wood dining table or a life-size religious effigy. Dealers range from the professional to the chaotic, although most are clued up about their prices. Most close for a 2-hour lunch, but once a year at the end of September they open for 24 hours. Traditional glassware, ceramics and original *azulejos* (tiles) taken from churches and renovated buildings can also be purchased. There is also a number of good contemporary design shops.

Rua de São Bento

Alma Lusa designer jewellery, clothes and quirky products

Brique a Braque de São Bento a curious treasure-trove of antique trinkets
Camara dos Pares a mixture of furnishings from the 19th century up until the 1930s
Cavalo de Pau wood furniture crafted on the premises, and Eastern-style *objets d'art*
Cinco 50 Zero retro 1950s, '60s and '70s furnishings and artwork
Deposito da Marinha Grande hand-blown glasswork in copies of old designs
Estantes and Moveis Oriental and Edwardian-inspired furnishings
Izu Interiors contemporary interior design and furnishings
Janelas de São Bento interior decorators with Edwardian-inspired, rather feminine furnishings
Jorge Welsh Oriental porcelain
Luis Lopes dusty antiques, chandeliers and crockery from the 18th and 19th centuries
Soc Comercial a Rocha traditional crafted glassware
Tempantigo specializes in ornate statues

Rua da Escola Politécnica

Arquitectonica minimalist furniture shop selling top grade designs
Fadas e Brava designer women's wear from Portuguese designers, and Eastern-inspired jewellery
Interna Emporio Casa modern interior design store selling household items, art books and bags

Rua Dom Pedro V

Galeria da Arcada mainly Portuguese religious carvings from 15th to the 19th centuries
Solar antique *azulejos* (tiles) arranged chronologically from the 15th to the 19th centuries

Rua do Século

O Espirito dos Coisas imported Eastern knick-knacks sold

from the owner's front room

Tom Tom Shop household wares and quirky design products.
A larger store over the road, housed in a former bakery and stables; sells renovated furniture and lamps.

SHOPPING CENTRES

Amoreiras, Avenida Engheiro Duarte Pacheco, Amoreiras.

The original one-stop shopping arcade, but its Brazilian design
now looks dated. Houses international chains, a cinema and a
health club.

Armazens do Chiado, Rua do Carmo, Chiado.

After it was destroyed by the 1988 fire, the reopening of this
downtown shopping centre was met with approval from the
city's youth. It houses FNAC (books, audio-visual, music),
Sephora (cosmetics) Massimo Dutti, Adolfo Dominguez, Ana
Sousa (young designer), Springfield, Sportszone and much more.

Centro Colombo, Avenida Lusiada, Benfica.

Lisbon's largest and most popular shopping complex, with a
number of high-street and designer concessions. Also a leisure
complex with health club, cinema, bowling alley and even a
chapel!

play...

Portugal isn't particularly known for its sporting prowess. Of all the spectator sports, football is the most popular, with Lisbon loyalties divided between Benfica and Sporting Lisboa. Thanks to the recent 2004 European Cup, both teams have newly renovated state-of-the-art grounds and a renewed enthusiasm for international football. Portugal's greatest sporting export is Luis Figo, who at one time was the world's most expensive player.

Bullfighting still commands a loyal following, although the city bullring at Campo Pequeno is currently closed for building work, but is due to reopen at the end of 2005. The Portuguese *tourada* (bullfight) is less popular and violent than its Spanish counterpart and the kill is strictly symbolic.

Some of Europe's finest golf courses can be found in Portugal, although they're all outside the city; most lie between Estoril and Sintra. Many hotels can arrange golfing expeditions on request and offer cut-price packages, which often prove cheaper than paying for an individual round. International golf week takes place in late October/early November. See www.portugalgolf.pt for more information.

Although Lisbon is surrounded by water, sailing facilities in the area are limited. The Terra Incognita Centro Nautico in Belém offers some of the best deals for boat hire (with a skipper), and windsurfing schools can be found further up the coast in Cascais and Guincho.

The areas of wide-open space around Lisbon lend themselves to activities such as horse-riding and even paintball. The latter has grown in popularity over the last few years and organizations can arrange group events on request.

As a rule, the Portuguese don't like to exercise. Gyms are a fairly recent phenomenon and the best clubs are owned by English companies such as Holmes Place and Clube VII. Most are happy to arrange a day pass for non-members.

As far as spas go, there is a similar gaping hole in the market, although heavy-weight hotels are gradually waking up to this fact and investing in new health clubs. Some of the best facilities can be found here, and a few are open to non-residents. Alternatively, many of the city gyms also offer beauty treatments.

BULLFIGHTING

Campo Pequeno, Praça de Touros do Campo Pequeno.
Tel: 21 793 2143

This Moorish-style arena, built in 1892, is one of the oldest bull-
rings in Europe. The season generally lasts from April to
September and tickets cost between €15 and €60, depending on
whether you opt for *sol* (sunny) or *sombra* (shady) seating. Unlike
Spanish fights, the bull is not killed (although it often dies out of
sight afterwards). The *tourada* opens with a *toureiro* in 18th-
century costume provoking the bull. An eight-man-team of
forcados then moves in to immobilize the animal. Finally they
persuade the bull to charge at them, while the front man leaps
between the horns. The Lusitano horse, able literally to run rings
around the bull with graceful prowess, is key to this process.
Building work on an underground car park has seen the ring
closed for the past two years, but if you're keen for the experience, bullfights regularly take place in the small towns around
Ribatejo (north-west of Lisbon), where the animals are bred.

FISHING

Sea fishing is free and grey mullet, sea bream, squid and sea bass
can be caught along the coast from Oeiras to Cascais. River fishing requires a licence which can be purchased from the
Direcção-Geral das Florestas (Avenida João Crisostomo, 26–28,
Saldanha), although few people bother. Contact the Federação
Portuguesa de Pesca Desportiva (tel: 21 356 3147) for advice on
fishing in Portuguese rivers.

FOOTBALL

There are three football teams in Lisbon: Benfica and Sporting
are both regulars on the European circuit, while Belenenses of
Belem is a smaller, First Division team. The season runs from
September to mid-June, and most league games are held on a
Sunday, with bigger international or cup games on Friday,
Sunday or Monday evenings. Fixtures can be found in *Bola*, the

daily soccer tabloid, at www.portuguesesoccer.com or
www.infodesporto.pt/futebal. Tickets for big games cost anything
from €3 to €30 and can be purchased in advance at the ABEP
kiosk in Praca dos Restauradores (for a handling fee) or at the
grounds on the night.

Sport Lisboa e Benfica, Estadio da Luz, Avenida General Norton de Matos.
Tel: 21 726 6129 www.slbenfica.pt

Benfica is Lisbon's most famous team, having won the Portuguese
championship and the Portuguese cup over 20 times. They were
also European champions in 1961/62. In recent years the club
has experienced a number of financial and management problems. Their newly renovated stadium north of the city played
main host to the 2004 European championships.

Sporting Club de Portugal, Estadio de Alvalade, Rua Francisco Stromp, Alvalade.
Tel: 21 751 4000 www.sporting.pt

Traditional rivals to Benfica, Sporting Lisbon enjoyed a degree of
success when they won the championship for the first time in 20
years, in 2000. Since then their performance has much improved.
Their new stadium was built for the 2004 European
Championships.

GOLF

Belas Clube de Campo, Alameda do Aqueducto, Belas Clube de Campo.
Tel: 21 962 6130

Set against the rolling hills of Sintra, the Belas golf club is a 20-
minute drive from Lisbon. Designed by revered golf course architect 'Rocky' Roquemor, it has five lakes with various picturesque
watercourses. The 18-hole, 6,380m, par-72 course also has a
driving range, two practice putting greens and clubhouse facilities

for a championship course. Take the A5 from Lisbon and head towards Sintra on the EN117.

Estoril Sol, Estrada da Lagoa Azul, Linho, Sintra.
Tel: 21 923 2461

Close to Quinta da Beloura, this nine-hole (par-33) course is one of the most beautiful in Europe. There's also a fantastic training ground for improvement of all areas of the game, a driving-range, putting green, restaurant, bar, open-air café and golf shop.

Golfe do Estoril, Avenida da Republica 2765, Estoril.
Tel: 21 468 0176

Close to the Estoril resort, the Portuguese Open was held here between 1953 and 1972 and again in 1987. Uneven terrain makes the 18-hole (par-69) course a challenge for golfers. The first nine holes were designed by Jean Gassiat in 1929 and the rest later completed by Mackenzie Ross; the 16th is considered to be the best hole in Portugal. It's members-only at weekends, although non-members can use a nine-hole (par-34) course. The A5 motorway now crosses the course. Facilities include a driving-range, putting green, restaurant, bar, swimming pool and golf shop. Take the Estoril exit on the A5 and follow signs to Sintra.

Lisbon Sports Club, Casal da Carregueira, Belas, Queluz.
Tel: 21 432 1474

Over the road from the Belas golf club, this 18-hole (par 69) course is far trickier. Crossed by the River Jamor, 12 of the 18 holes are influenced by water hazards. Founded by British ex-pats in 1922, this is the second-oldest course in Portugal. Club facilities include tennis courts, a swimming pool and sauna.

Quinta da Beloura, Estrada da Albarraque, Sintra.
Tel: 21 910 6350

Located between Cascais and Sintra, this 35-acre 18-hole (par-

69) flat course has fantastic panoramic hill views. The green is lined with 40,000 trees, and the 16th and 17th holes are separated by a lake. Facilities include a driving range, putting green and restaurant.

Quinta da Marinha, Quinta da Marinha, Cascais.
Tel: 21 486 0108

Located 25km from Lisbon, overlooking the Guincho beach, this flat 18-hole (par-71) course is famous for its 13th hole with a par 4 that plunges towards the sea. The 14th hole (set behind a cliff) and 10th hole (whose green is surrounded by water) will also test the limits of an experienced golfer. Facilities include a driving range, swimming pools, tennis courts, restaurants and a hotel.

Quinta da Penha Longa, Quinta da Penha Longa, Estrada da Lagoa Azul, Linho, Sintra.
Tel: 21 924 9000

Considered to be one of the best greens in Europe, this 18-hole course was designed by Robert Trent Jones Jr. The club has a hotel, two putting greens, two driving ranges, restaurant, bar, golf shop, sauna and jacuzzi. An adjacent nine-hole (par-35) course is less hilly and played host to the 1994 and 1995 Portuguese Open. The Mosteiro takes its name from the nearby Penha Longa monastery. Greens are fast and the fairways narrow. Take the EN9 Estoril–Sintra road and turn left at signs for Lagoa Azul.

GYMS

Barriga Killer, Rua Cintura do Porto, Armazém J, Santos.
Tel: 21 395 6428
Open: 8am–10pm Monday–Friday; 11am–4pm Saturday; 11am–3pm Sunday

Housed in a converted warehouse on the docks, this club offers aerobics, step, weights, sauna and a Turkish bath.

Clube VII, Parque Eduardo VII, Rato.
Tel: 21 384 8300/1
Open: 7am–10pm daily

The English-owned outfit is the biggest and best-equipped private health club in Lisbon and can be found behind the busy Marques de Pombal roundabout at the top end of the Avenida da Liberdade. Facilities include eight tennis courts, one squash court, over 150 fitness classes, a 25m pool and gym. A number of beauty treatments and massages can also be booked. Membership is required, although day and week passes can be purchased. A reduced rate is also offered to guests staying at the Le Meridien hotel opposite. A day pass costs €33, or €115 for a week.

Health Club Solinca, Centro Colombo, loja A201, Avenida Lusiada.
Tel: 21 711 3650
Open: 7am–10pm Monday–Friday; 9am–8pm Saturday–Sunday

Part of the mammoth Colombo shopping centre, this modern gym offers classes in aerobics, step and yoga, along with a weights gym, solarium and massage centre.

Holmes Place, Avenida da Liberdade 38, Avenida.
Tel: 21 326 0900 www.holmesplace.com
Open: 7am–10pm Monday–Saturday; 10am–6pm Sunday

Part of the UK fitness chain, Holmes Place is considered one of the more exclusive clubs in Lisbon. Facilities include a swimming pool, gym, sauna, steam room, solarium, body and skin clinic and hair salon. The branch at Avenida Defonsores de Chaves 45 has a swimming pool with a retractable roof.

HORSE-RIDING

Centro Hipico da Costa do Estoril, Estrada da Charneca 186, Cascais.
Tel: 21 487 2064

Lessons are offered for riders of all abilities – in dressage and show jumping – and cost from €15. Two-hour treks to Monseratte and Capuchos with a guide cost €40. Friendly staff speak several languages.

Escola de Equitação Quinta da Marinha, Birre, Cascais.
Tel: 21 486 9282

This riding school has over 400 horses and can arrange trips in the Guincho-Cascais area or the Sintra hills. Lessons cost approximately €20 an hour.

Hipodromo do Campo Grande, Campo Grande.
Tel: 21 797 9465

Two annual dressage events take place in Lisbon. The Internacional Concurso Oficial de Saltos (which includes a Nations Cup) takes place in May at the Hipodromo do Campo Grande and lasts four days. Also held at the Hipodromo, the Festival Internacional do Cavalho Puro Sangue Lusitano takes place in June. The Lusitano, native to south-western Iberia, is the oldest saddle-horse in the world.

PAINTBALL AND LASERQUEST

Combatelaser, Nomadas, Turismo de Aventura lda.
Tel: 21 982 1128 www.combatelaser.com

A bit like paintball without the paint or a battle without the bullets, this seek-and-destroy combat game uses infra-red lasers similar to those on a TV remote control. Events take place in Lisbon's sprawling Monsanto woodland and currently only private sessions can be arranged for groups of 10 or more. The cost for a game (including insurance) is €25 per player.

Megacampo, Rua Arthilharia Um 67.
Tel: 21 386 3637 www.estratego.pt

Billing itself as the best paintball adventure centre on the Iberian peninsula, this 40-hectare complex has several differently themed courses, including Wild West Village and Fort Apache. The annual Portuguese Paintball Open is also held here. Check the website for more events. It's a 30-minute drive from Lisbon.

SAILING

Escola de Vela da Lagoa d'Óbidos, Foz do Arelho/Nadadouro.
Tel: 26 297 8592

A little further out of town, this school is set in a tranquil lagoon and offers windsurfing, catamaran, kayak and canoeing classes and rental. Take the A8 towards Leira, exit at Foz do Arelho and pick up the road signposted 'marginal da Lagoa'.

Proiate, Rua do Ferragial 7, Cais do Sodré.
Tel: 21 342 6877

Five yachts to rent in the Gib'Sea and Jeanneau ranges.

Terra Incognita Centro Nautico, Doca do Bom Sucesso, Ed. Vela Latina, Loja Exterior.
Tel: 21 302 1588 www.terraincognita.pt

Ten Beneto boats can be rented (with a skipper) from this sailing school in Belem. Sailing courses ranging from 4 hours to a week can be arranged for a minimum of five people. Requests for boat hire should be sent to info@terraincognita.pt.

SPAS

The culture for day spas and beauty treatment centres is yet to catch on in Lisbon and facilities are fairly thin on the ground. Most are either attached to hotel complexes or the city's similarly limited health clubs (see 'Gyms'); the best being Clube VII, which offers facials, manicures, massage and a comprehensive

range of beauty treatments. Below are listed hotels with spa
facilities open to non-residents.

Hotel Altis, Rua Castilho 11.

Tel: 21 310 6000 www.hotel-altis.pt
Open: 8am–9pm Monday–Friday; 10am–7pm Saturday–Sunday

Although slightly dated and in need of renovation, the Altis
Health Club is convenient, located just off the Avenida da
Liberdade. Facilities include a sauna, solarium, Turkish bath, massage and physiotherapy. A massage costs €40 for an hour.

Hotel Real Palácio, Rua Thomas Ribeiro 115.

Tel: 21 319 9500 www.hoteisreal.com
Open: 9am–9pm daily

Introduced as part of the hotel renovation, this tastefully
designed health club has good facilities, including a sauna, Turkish
baths and massage. A 50-minute aromatherapy massage costs
€45.

Hotel Vila Galé Opera, Travessa Conde da Ponte.

Tel: 21 360 5400
Open: 7.30am–10.30pm Monday–Friday; 11am–2pm Saturday.
Closed Sunday.

This modern health club has a swimming pool and gym facilities.
Treatments include Chinese therapy, acupuncture, massage,
sauna, Turkish bath and jacuzzi. A massage costs €45 for an hour.

info...

CAR HIRE

To rent a car in Portugal, drivers must be over 21 and have had a licence for more than one year. It is often cheaper to arrange a deal with travel agents beforehand, but cars can be hired once in the city.

CLIMATE

Lisbon's summers last from June to October and are largely dry; temperatures can reach 40°C, although a cool Atlantic breeze provides refreshing relief. Most Lisboetas take their holidays in July and August, leaving many shops and restaurants closed. Winters (December to February) are mild and temperatures rarely dip below 10°. However, rainfall can be high. Weather conditions are also extremely localized.

CRIME

Lisbon is a fairly safe city, and walking around should pose no real threat. However, it's still important to look out for pickpockets on public transport and to take care in areas such as the Alfama, the top of the Avenida da Liberdade and the streets around Martim Moniz after dark. The Portuguese government has decriminalized the use of soft drugs, although dealing still holds a heavy penalty. Drug-related crime tends to occur in the poorer suburbs and peripheral shanty-towns. If you are robbed, go to the tourist police station in Palácio Foz, Praça dos Restauradores (tel: 21 342 1634) to file a report, necessary for insurance claims.

EMERGENCIES

Call 112 for emergency services and specify either *policia*, *ambulancia* or *bombeiros* (fire brigade).

LISBOA CARDS

Several cards can be purchased from the tourist office offering visitors generous discounts. The Lisboa Card gives free public transport, access to 27 museums and monuments, and other reductions. These cards can be purchased for

periods of between 24 and 72 hours, and cost from €11.25 to €23.50. The Lisboa Shopping Card gives discounts of up to 20% in many of the city's key shops and the Lisboa Restaurant Card offers reductions in more than 40 restaurants. Cards can be purchased from the tourist office.

METRO

Lisbon's *metropolitano* is the best way to reach out-of-town destinations, such as the Expo '98 site at Parques de Nações (Oriente). Hours of operation are from 6.30am to 1am. Check www.metrolisboa.pt for more information. Many of the stations' interiors are themed, and make for fun viewing – the best is Antonio Da Costa's rabbit from *Alice in Wonderland*, who announces 'I'm late'.

TAXIS

Taxis are easy to come by in Lisbon and are reasonably priced: a minimum charge of €1.80 applies during the day, and €2.10 from 10pm to 6am and on weekends. It's easy to flag down taxis in the street, although rush hours can be busy. Ranks can be found at the bottom of Rossio, in Praça da Figueira, at Praça do Comercio and at the bottom of Avenida de Dom Carlos I. Alternatively they can be booked from Radio Taxis (tel: 21 811 9000), Autocoope (tel: 21 793 2756) or Teletaxi (tel: 21 811 1100). Lisbon's taxi drivers are famous for their attempts to rip off tourists, especially from the airport on arrival. For long journeys always agree a fixed price in advance and make sure the taxi has a meter. A trip from the airport should cost no more than €15. A taxi voucher, which guarantees a standard price, can be purchased from Lisbon airport at the tourist information counters. Tipping is optional, although many grumpy drivers consider it an obligation.

TELEPHONE

To phone Lisbon from abroad dial 00 + 351 (country code) + nine-digit number. To phone abroad from Lisbon dial 00 + country code (UK 44) + area code (minus initial 0) + number.

info...

TIPPING

A standard tip of 10% is normal in cafés and restaurants, but not necessarily bars. Taxi drivers expect a tip but this is at your discretion.

TOURIST INFORMATION

Lisboa Welcome Centre, Rua do Arsenal 15, Baixa.
Tel: 21 031 2700 www.atl-turismolisboa.pt
Open: 9am–8pm daily.
Useful for general information.

Turismo, Palácio Foz, Praça dos Restauradores, Baixa.
Tel: 21 346 3314 www.portugalinsite.pt
Open: 9am–8pm daily.
Supplies accommodation lists, bus timetables and maps. A free telephone information line gives information in English (9am–midnight Monday–Saturday; 9am–8pm Sunday), tel: 800 296 296. *Follow Me Lisboa* and *Lisboa Step by Step* are both free listings magazines, available from the tourist office.

TRAMS AND BUSES

Trams are probably the most romantic way to see Lisbon, but by no means the quickest. The most picturesque routes are the cross-city 28, which winds its way through the steep streets of Graça, and the 12, which circles the castle area east of the city centre, via Alfama, Praça da Figueira and Largo Martim Moniz.

Bus routes are particularly comprehensive (most buses can be picked up at Praça do Comercio), and the city's four funiculars (*elevadores*) save back-breaking hikes up some of the steepest streets. All tickets can be purchased on board, but are cheaper if bought in advance from kiosks in Praça do Comercio and Praça da Figueira. A one-day *Bilhete Turistico* (tourist ticket) costs €2.50 and allows unlimited travel.

index

Adult entertainment 165–7
Champagne Club 165–6
Savana Club 166
Show Girls 166–7
Alcântara see
Lapa/Alcântara/Belém
Alfama see
Graça/Sé/Alfama
architecture 169
Avenida da Liberdade 16, 28, 184–5
Avenida/Rato/Estrêla 16–19
map 18–19

Baixa/Bairro Alto 8, 12–16
bars 13, 98–9
cafés 125
map 14–15
restaurants 12, 58
shopping 12, 13, 182, 185–7
bars 98–123
121, Rua do Norte 100
Agito 100–1
Bairro Alto area 13, 98–9
Baliza 101–2
and beer-drinking 99
Berim Bar 102–3
Bicaense 103
Café de São Bento 103–4, 123
Cafédiário 98, 104–5
Caxim Bar 105–6
Clube da Esquina 106
Costa do Castelo Bar das Imagens 106–7
Divina Comédia 107–8
Esplanada do Rio 108–9
Estado Liquido 109
Fluid 110
Fragil 98, 99, 110–11
Herois 111–12
Lapa/Alcântara/Belém area 24
Lounge Café 112–13
Lua 113
Madres de Goa 113–14
Majong 114–15
Mexe 115–16
Net Jazz Café 70, 116
O'Gilin's 99, 116–17
Paródia 99, 117–18
Pavilhão Chinês 99, 118–19

Perudiguous do Rio 119
Portas Largas 120
Procópio 99, 120–1
Santiago Alquimista 121
Side 13, 122–3
Snob 123
Belém see
Lapa/Alcântara/Belém
Benfica stadium 50
Branco, Cassiano 38
bullfighting 194, 196
buses 206

cafés 124–47
Alcântara 77
Arte Café 126–7
As Vicentinhas 127–8
Baliza 125
Buenas Aires 128–9
Café Bernard 129
Café a Brasíliera 12, 125, 130
Café Nicola 125, 130–1
Café no Chiado 125, 131–2
Café no Combro 132–3
Café Rosso 133
Café Suiça 133–4
cakes 124
Cerca Moura 134–5
coffee 124
Crazy Nuts 136
Cultura do Cha 125, 136–7
Esplanada 137–8
Esplanada da Graça 138–9
Esplanada do Adamastor 139
Madres de Goa 125
Martinho da Arcada 125, 139–40
O Cha da Lapa 140–1
O Outra Face da Lua 141–2
Pão de Canela 142
Pastelaria Versailles 143–4
Pastelaria-Padaria São Roque 144–5
Pâu de Canela 125
SV Café 145
Teatro Taborda 146
Verde Perto 146–7
Versailles 125
cake shops 124
Antiga Confeitaria de Belém 126

Confeitaria Nacional 135–6
Pasteis de Cerveja 143
Campo de Ourique 17
Campo de Santa Clara 21
car hire 204
Castelo de São Jorge 9, 20, 21, 169, 170
Solar do Castelo hotel 20, 29, 30, 51–2
Chapitô circus school 21, 107, 178–9
Chiado district 12–13, 125, 183
climate 204
Coelho, Luis Pinto 99, 117
Columbus, Christopher 25
Convento do Carmo 171–2
Costa do Castelo road 21
Coustols, Frederic P. 48–9
crime 204

drugs 149, 204

earthquake (1755) 12, 13, 48, 168, 172
Eduardo VII park 16, 36, 46
Elevador da Santa Justa 172
emergencies 204
esplanadas 125, 138–9
Estrêla see
Avenida/Rato/Estrêla
Euro 2004 football championships 8, 194
Experimenta Design Biennale exhibition 168
Expo '98 site 8, 168, 205

fado houses 13, 21, 83, 149, 162, 163–4
Feira da Ladra flea market 21, 78
Figo, Luis 194
Figugirdo, Joaquim 94
fishing 196
football 8, 194, 196–7

Gama, Vasco da 25, 174
Gemelli, Augusto 74
golf 194, 197–9
Graça/Sé/Alfama 9, 20–3
bars 20
hotels 20–1
map 22–3
restaurants 20
Greene, Graham 57

Gulbenkian Foundation 168, 179–80
gyms 195, 199–200

Hallin, Elena 66–7
Henry the Navigator 169
history 168–9
horse-riding 195, 200–1
hotels 28–57
Albergaria Senhora Do Monte 31
As Janelas Verdes 24, 31–2
Avenida da Liberdade 16, 28
Avenida Palace 28, 30, 32–3
Carlton Pestana Palace 28, 30, 33–4
chains 28, 29
Don Pedro Hotel Lisboa 34–5
Fenix Lisboa 28, 35
Four Seasons Hotel Ritz 28, 30, 36–7
Graça/Sé/Alfama area 20–1
Hoteis Heritage 29
Hotel Altis 37–8
Hotel Britania 29, 38–9
Hotel Lisboa Plaza 39–40
Hotel Metrópole 40–1
Hotel Venezia 42
Janelas Verdes 42
Lapa Palace 24, 28, 30, 43
Lapa/Alcântara/Belém area 24
Lisboa Palace 29
Lisboa Regency Chiado 29, 30, 44
Lisboa Tejo Hotel 29, 30, 45
Meridian Park Atlantic 28, 45–6
Metrópole 30
NH Liberade 28, 30, 46–7
Olissipo 47–8
Palácio Belmonte 21, 28, 30, 48–9
Quinta Nova da Conceição 29, 30, 49–50
Real Palácio 28, 41, 203
Sheraton Lisboa 50–1
Solar do Castelo 20, 29, 30, 51–2

207

Hg2 Lisbon

index

Solar dos Mouros 29, 30, 52–3
spa facilities 203
style, location and atmosphere 30
Tivoli Jardim 53–4
Tivoli Lisboa 54–5
top ten 30
Vila Galé Opera 55–6, 203
VIP Eden 30, 56
York House 24, 30, 57

Jardim da Estrela 17
Jardim das Amoreiras 17
Jardim do Ultramarino 25
jazz clubs 16, 162–3, 164–5
José, Herman 62

Lapa/Alcântara/Belém 9, 24–7
Antiga Casa de Pasteis de Belém 25, 126
bars 24
hotels 24
map 26–7
nightclubs 24
Pasteis de Cerveja 25
restaurants 24
shopping 25
laserquest 201–2
Le Carré, John 57
Lemos, Luis 52
Lisboa Cards 204–5
Livraria Bertrand 12

Mãe de Agua 173
Malkovich, John 21, 66, 148
maps
Avenida/Rato/Estrêla 18–19
Baixa/Bairro Alto 14–15
Graça/Sé/Alfama 22–3
Lapa/Alcântara/Belém 26–7
Lisbon city 10–11
metro 205
Monsanto forest 25
Mosteiro dos Jerónimos 173–4
Museu do Design 174–5
museums and galleries
Centro de Arte Moderna 170–1
Museu do Design 174–5
Museu Nacional do Azulejo 175–6
music clubs 149, 162–5
fado houses 13, 21, 83, 149, 162, 163–4

Hot Clube 16, 162–3
Net Jazz 149
Senhor Vinho 163–4
Speakeasy 164–5

nightclubs 148–9, 150–62
B. Leza 149, 150–1
BBC 148, 150
Convento 151
Docks Club 148, 152
doormen 149
Incógnito 153
Kapital 24, 77, 148, 153–4
Kremlin 24, 77, 154–5
Lapa/Alcântara/Belém 24
Lontra 149, 155–6
Lux 21, 66, 148, 156–7
O2Lx 148, 157
Op Art 148, 158
Paradise Grange 148, 158–9
People 159–60
Queens 148, 160
Rocha Conde d'Obidos 24
W 161–2
Nunes, Carlos Cabral 127

Ocenarium 176

Pacheco, Mario 162
Padrão dos Descobrimentos (Monument to the Discoveries) 25
paintball 195, 201–2
Paola, Maria 68
Parque Eduardo VII 16, 36, 46
Pessoa, Fernando 12, 16, 17, 130
Pina, Massa 35
Pinto, Antonio 62
Pombal, Marquês de 12, 169
Ponte 25 de Abril suspension bridge 24
Praca da Alegria 16
Praca das Flores 17
Praça do Comercio 25
Praca Dom Pedro IV (Rossio) 12, 40, 99
Principe Real 16–17

Queiros, Eça de 31–2
Queiroz, Francisco 91

Rato see Avenida/Rato/Estrêla
Reis, Manuel 21, 99, 111, 148, 156

restaurants 9, 58–97
1 de Maio 58, 61
A Picanha 63
A Travessa 59, 60, 63–4
Alcântara Café 62
Aya 58, 64–5
Baixa/Bairro Alto area 12, 58
Bica do Sapato 21, 60, 65–6, 98
Bolshoi 59, 60, 66–7
Casa Nostra 67–8
Casanova 58, 68–9
Chapitô 60, 69–70
Charcuteria 70–1
El Gordo 71–2
Enoteca 59, 72–3
Estufa Real 59, 73–4
food, service and atmosphere 60
Galeria 60, 74–5
Galeto 75
Gambrinus 59, 60, 76
Graça/Sé/Alfama area 60
Kais 59, 60, 76–7, 98
Lapa/Alcântara/Belém 24
Lisboa Noite 77–8, 98
local specialities 58
Mercado de Santa Clara 59, 78–9
Mezza Luna 79–80
Nariz Apurado 80–1
Nariz do Vinho Tinto 81–2
Oliviers 58, 60, 82–3
Os Corvos 60, 83–4
Pap' Açorda 59, 84–5
Pinoquio 85
Porco Pretto 86
Primavera 58, 86–7
Ramiro 59, 87–8
Santo Antonio 88–9
Sinal Vermelho 58, 89–90
Solar dos Nunes 58, 90–1
style, location and atmosphere 60
Sua Excelência 59, 60, 91–2
Sushi Bar 92–3
Tasquina da Adelaide 17, 58, 60, 93–4
Tavares Rico 94–5
top ten 60
Valle Flor, Hotel Carlton Pestana Palace 34
Varanda, Four Seasons Ritz Hotel 36, 95
Viagem de Sabores 96

wine 59
XL 17, 60, 96–7
York House 57
Ribeiro, Antonio 12–13
Rossio (Praca Dom Pedro IV) 12, 40, 99
Rua do Diário de Notícias 13, 98

sailing 195, 202
Salazar, Olveira 36, 169
Santa Apólonia development 21
Sao Bento area 17
Sé see Graça/Sé/Alfama
Sé cathedral 20, 96
shopping 12, 13, 25, 182–93
Avenida da Liberdade 184–5
Bairro Alto 13, 187–8
Baixa 12, 182, 185–7
centres 193
Chiado 13, 183, 188–90
fashion 183
opening hours 183
Santa Apolonia 190–1
São Bento/Rato 17, 191–3
traditional crafts 182–3
sightseeing 25, 170–7
spas 36, 195, 202–3
strip-clubs 16, 149, 165–7

Tarantino, Quentin 75
taxis 205
telephone 205
theatres
CCB (Centro Cultural de Belém) 25, 168, 177–8
Coliseu dos Recreios 179
Gulbenkian Foundation 168, 179–80
Nacional Teatro Dona Maria II 168, 181
Teatro Luis de Camoes 168
Teatro Nacional de São Carlos 168, 180
tipping 206
Torré de Belém 25, 177
tourist information 206
trams 206

Viera, Alvaro Siza 13
Viterbo, Graça 39, 41

windsurfing 195